Praise fo

'Joe Gisbey's interesting an[...]
you back into the world of J[...]
factions and racial jealousies, [...] ...ervour and
fanatical terrorism. But it doesn't leave you there—it
brings Jesus' teaching right back into your here and
now. Read on and prepare to be challenged!'

Rev. Dr William Atkinson, Senior Lecturer in
Pentecostal and Charismatic Studies,
London School of Theology

'This is Joe's first book but it will certainly not be the last.
Joe has an amazing understanding of Jewish culture and
has an outstanding ability to put that into the context
of Christ's ministry. He opens up the journey of Jesus
on the earth like no one else that I know. His story is
uniquely his and he has been on a journey of faith that
enables him to be an outstanding Bible teacher. As he
walks through the story of Jesus the rabbi, walk with him
and be challenged and inspired. I know that you will see
the life of Jesus in a new way and a fresh light.'

Norman Barnes, Founder, Links International

'This is the moment that God has called us to raise up
a generation that follows Jesus in every area of their
lives. I am certain that this book will both help you
and challenge you to be a true disciple of our master.
We got to know Joe during his time in Colombia and
what greatly impacted us was the passion within his
heart for God and in turn God's loving compassion

within him for people. His testimony is an inspiration to us all and shows that it is so worth it, to follow the footsteps of our great master, Jesus!'

Pastor Johanna Castellanos, Leader, G12 Movement and the International Charismatic Mission Church, Bogotá, Colombia

'Having known Joe since he was in short trousers, it's been incredible to see his life's journey unfold. I see him now as someone who has a great ability to hold in tension the theological understanding of scripture, its practical application, and not least a prophetic understanding of God's heart for the local church – a huge gift that few attain. Joe's life story is in itself compelling, but he would be the first to say that the greatest story of all remains the one of God meeting and transforming us all through a relationship with Jesus.'

Tim Jupp, CEO and Founder, Big Church Day Out

'Joe's story shows that God can take anyone, no matter how far they might have walked away from him, and use them for his kingdom. When we walk close enough to get covered in his dust, amazing things are sure to follow.'

Billy Kennedy, Leader, Pioneer Network

'Joe is the real deal. He lives out what he talks about. This book is a unique message to all those who want to be a friend of God.'

Martin Smith, singer and songwriter

FOLLOW

WALKING IN THE DUST OF THE RABBI

FOLLOW

WALKING IN THE DUST OF THE RABBI

JOSEPH GISBEY

DARTON·LONGMAN + TODD

First published in 2015 by Darton, Longman and Todd Ltd
1 Spencer Court
140–142 Wandsworth High Street
London SW18 4JJ

ISBN 978-0-232-53165-7

A catalogue record for this book is available from the British Library.

Designed and typeset by Judy Linard
Printed and bound in Great Britain by Bell & Bain, Glasgow

DEDICATION

First and foremost, I dedicate this to my saviour Jesus – my Rabbi, whose dust I pray will always cover me as I aim to follow in his footsteps.

Then to my beautiful wife Carolina, who has stood by me and constantly inspired and challenged me to put pen to paper and share these stories. You are my inspiration. Also to my four amazing children, Luca, Elyana, Zion and Seth, who have been willing to share their dad with many people and places around the world.

To my beautiful, inspiring parents Mick and Chrissy Gisbey, my siblings Ben, Beth and Miriam and my church family at Arun Community Church – ordinary radicals and history-makers, who both prayed me through my darkest moments and cheered me on through God's amazing healing and the adventures that have since ensued. It is such an honour and privilege to journey with you all. Together we're seeing the world transformed and heaven breaking out on earth.

Finally, I must thank my grandparents Albert and June Mosedale, who instilled in me a passion for the Jewish roots of our faith and a deep love for Israel. Your love and wisdom flow through the DNA of this book. Grandad, you are now dancing and kicking up the dust

FOLLOW

from the golden streets of the heavenly Jerusalem. We love and miss you. May we all follow and walk in the dust of the Rabbi as you did.

CONTENTS

INTRODUCTION

This is a book about what I believe it means to follow Jesus, to really be a disciple. It is a glance at the world of Jesus, comparing it with our twenty-first century world, where we see the lines blurred and what we might have imagined as two very diverse cultures actually having more in common than at first glance. It is about a heart cry to know God and make him known, to pursue him with reckless abandon wherever he leads, to be so close to the heart of God that the world would take note that we have been with Jesus.

Some years ago I was with my kids in Parque Bolivar in Bogotá, the capital city of Colombia, having followed God's heart to start a community of faith in some of the most difficult communities of this amazing nation. We were waiting for the grand finale of the G12 convention, that this year had been called *Pintando la ciudad de Rojo* ('painting the city red'.) This title had been inspired by a song written by a friend, who had in turn been inspired by the statement of an evangelist who holds very large crusades on the continent of Africa.

The red we paint with is the blood of Jesus. That blood brings freedom and liberty, washes us whiter than snow, and breaks the chains of pain, sickness, injustice and poverty.

11

That blood speaks of better things than the blood of Abel, not of judgement but rather of mercy.

In a few hours everyone would be singing and proclaiming that they were on their way to 'paint this big old town red, with the blood of Jesus'. The song has a football hooligan element to it, a rebelling against the system of this present darkness and a rising up to do some holy mischief. We're going out to paint, but it's going to be graffiti, there's going to be some vandalism and breaking down of the enemy's strongholds.

It got me thinking about the way we are taught to paint. When Luca, my oldest son, was in his transition year of play school, getting ready for big school, he often brought home pictures he had to colour or paint. The mortal sin, destined to bring little red error crosses in all their fury onto his workbook, was if he went outside the lines! And so very carefully he followed the rules, slowly filling in the blank with colour; occasionally there was a paint/colour by numbers, restricting that creative fire within even further. You could see the frustration in his eyes as he desired to paint the elephant green, his favourite colour, and in his thinking, why couldn't an elephant be green? Creativity bubbles inside us; at our core we are all artisans. Our souls long to create, to push boundaries and throw off the limitations. The feminist philosopher Mary Daly said, 'It is the creative potential itself in human beings that is the image of God' and she is absolutely right. We are acting out our God-given potential, his fingerprint on our lives, when we break out of the box of conformity.

Don't get me wrong – there is a time and a place for rules, structure and taking care. However, sometimes we grow up with that drilled in so deeply that we lose the desire to allow our creativity to soar; to draw a round house, rather than a square one, a blazing fiery ball of reds, oranges and yellows to express the sun instead of a perfect circle with ruler-lined rays being emitted into a blue, cloudless sky.

In Parque Bolivar it was beginning to look ominous overhead, as dark looming clouds began to gather and everyone from the event's organisers to the sellers of various fast food fancies to keep the masses' tummies full was looking rather concerned. The weather is very unpredictable there. The only thing that is predictable is that it will be unpredictable. Moments before, the sun had been scorching and we had enjoyed an ice cream while sitting on the bouncy Andean grass. Elyana, my little princess, who was three at the time, lay back, ice cream covering her face, and looked up at the clouds. 'Look, Daddy,' she said, pointing up at a towering fluffy white cumulonimbus, 'there's the castle'. I looked up intently, half expecting to see a castle because of the certainty in her voice, 'Which castle, honey?' I replied. 'The Jack one, with the giant, you see it, you see it?' It was clear she did, even if I couldn't. Soon we were playing that age-old game of seeing images within the clouds. It's fascinating that a number of people can look up and see the same cloud and all will see something different and new. Same cloud, different perspective.

I am a husband to an amazing woman and now father to four incredible children. I am a pastor, and that last one seems to sometimes get people a little nervous. However, I am just like anyone else, trying to work it out, fragile and broken. I laugh a lot, I cry a lot, I have a lot of fun – sometimes too much fun! Yet, like us all, one moment I can be lost in self-loathing, the next flaunting my self-righteousness. I have been lost beyond belief and I have been gloriously rescued. At sixteen years of age Jesus took me and saved me from the point of death, and since that amazing encounter I have been privileged to travel to more than forty nations to see God move in incredible and powerful ways. He has allowed me both to start churches and to be involved in amazing communities. We have seen many thousands break free from poverty, many healed and many lives transformed. All this has simply been the side effect of following Jesus, being close enough to be, as the ancient Rabbis would say, 'covered in his dust'. Here in Bogotá, Colombia we were getting pretty dusty that day!

In the distance I could hear the practice coming to an end and people beginning to file into the park – there would be tens of thousands here soon, of different ages, colours, characters and backgrounds but gathering around a common story and a common cause. We've all been mesmerised by the cloud. We see different elements of it but ultimately we are gathering around the cloud by day and the fire by night. We are artists getting ready to paint, God's poetry in motion, players on God's great stage. We are tired of painting by numbers, not colouring outside the lines – here we come, covered in the dust of the Rabbi, to rediscover the wonder, reimagine the possibilities and repaint this big old whitewashed town we call Christendom with the blood of Jesus.

FOLLOW

WALKING IN THE DUST OF THE RABBI

CHAPTER 1

HEWN FROM THE ROCK

The smell of hummus and freshly baked bread mingled with the perfumes and spices as I made my way through the narrow winding streets of Cairo. It was a feast for the eyes – colours everywhere, smells of food cooking, garbage being burnt, the Arabian nights music from Disney's Aladdin *playing in my head. I was on my way to see an ancient Coptic church that had been built into a huge rock face. It is found in an urban sector where the people are called* zabaleen *(literally 'garbage people'), and yet here in this grotto God was doing some remarkable miracles. Many people were receiving physical healings and there were even some rather bizarre signs and wonders going on, but aside from all this the community was being transformed. Goods were being recycled, beauty was found in the rubbish. The forgotten, the outcast, the garbage people who met in a church hewn out of the rock were turning their part of the world upside down.*

What a picture of the church. We have been hewn out of the rock, joined to a greater story. Jesus referred to us as the salt of the earth. You have probably heard it taught that salt flavours and purifies and this is absolutely true. However, to Jesus' audience salt had another obvious use, especially in rural, farming communities. There wasn't an abundance of wood for fuel so instead, sheep and goats' droppings would be used. They found out very early on that mixing salt into these droppings made them burn more strongly and for longer. Jesus' audience knew this all too well, and would most likely have recalled such a fact when hearing him teach this principle. Essentially Jesus was saying that we are to be mixed into the rubbish of this world and set it alight with the fire and passion of his Spirit. Fire purifies, fire transforms.

American president Woodrow Wilson understood that we are not here to simply go through life, to achieve, marry, have kids, buy a house, retire and check out. We are here to leave the world in a better state than we found it in. He once said: 'You are here in order to enable the world to live more amply, with greater vision, with a finer spirit of hope and achievement. You are here to enrich the world.' Who more than the children of God, heirs and stewards of this earth, should understand this fact?

Jesus never came to start an institution, nor did he have a religion in mind. He came to put into motion a movement of passion and power that would cover the globe like a flood. He came to make everything new. All that was lost in Eden was to be restored. People would be able to walk and talk with God again; the earth that had groaned and ached for so long would be released. Jesus came to show us how it could be done – how people could be infused with the very presence and glory of God.

I probably need to identify and clarify some core personal beliefs and statements, due to the slightly radical nature of some of the issues that we are going to journey

18

through together in this retelling of the ancient story we know as the gospel. Jesus was and is 100 per cent God, in human form. Colossians 1:15–18 says:

> He is the image of the invisible God, the firstborn over all creation. For by him all things were created: things in heaven and on earth, visible and invisible, whether thrones or powers or rulers or authorities; all things were created by him and for him. He is before all things, and in him all things hold together. And he is the head of the body, the church; he is the beginning and the firstborn from among the dead, so that in everything he might have the supremacy.

However, Jesus was also fully human. Jesus was Jewish. His world was dramatically different from the western world of today. Through the centuries we have cut ourselves off from the historical and geographical context of the roots of our faith, causing a lack of understanding of the scriptures. We open the pages of the first chapter of Matthew and forget that four hundred years have passed since the final words of the First Testament. To better understand the Gospels, we must first understand the sociology, history and geography of the land, its customs, tradition and culture. Jesus' words, actions and teaching methods were in keeping with the culture into which he was born. We must understand his words and actions in the light of his world.

Throughout this book we are going to look at Jesus in his role as a Jewish Rabbi of incredible talent and extraordinary insight. Most Christian disciplines have focused on the divinity of Christ, firstly because it was necessary to combat Gnostic teachings in the early church, but secondly, perhaps, because we may have a hard time accepting Jesus as fully human. 'You mean to say Jesus laughed, cried, liked a good slap-up meal and dare I say, a fine wine or cold beer after enjoying a swim in a cool brook in the heat of the day?' Absolutely! Jesus was human, Jewishly human, and very much in touch with his emotions. We might not feel comfortable with this Jesus, the Jesus that had to use the rest room, got tired, even angry at times. If we put Jesus on a pedestal and reason that he did the things he did because of his divinity, we may be giving ourselves a get-out clause for living the kind of life that he has called us to live.

Jesus himself said in the scriptures that 'Anyone who has faith in me will do what I have been doing. He will do even greater things than these, because I am going to the Father' (John 14:12). We look at everything that Jesus did with the attitude that, 'Well, of course Jesus can do those things; he is God.' I totally believe that Jesus is the king of kings and lord of lords, God all powerful, creator of heaven and earth. However, I also believe that everything that Jesus did during his ministry here on earth he did being fully human, showing us what God intended for us to be as flesh-and-blood sons and daughters of Adam and Eve, filled and imbibed with the power and presence of God. Partners in God's nature? Is that possible? I know my nature and it usually looks a lot more like Joe nature than Jesus nature. Can it be true that God believes we can fully embrace being human and at the same time, in Christ, walk in the divine? How do we wrestle with this idea of Jesus as fully human and fully God? Welcome to one of the greatest theological mazes of all time!

In Philippians 2:6–8 it says that Jesus, 'being in very nature God, did not consider equality with God something to be grasped, but made himself nothing, taking the very nature of a servant'. The term 'made himself nothing' is an attempt to translate the Greek term *kenoō*, which means to empty yourself of something or to lay it to one side and choose not to use it. The scriptures are saying that Jesus chose to put his identity as God on the shelf so that he could live a fully human life.

Obviously in many ways it is impossible to not see this as somewhat of a false separation – if Jesus is one person how can you take him apart? But Paul is trying to explain that although Jesus had the opportunity to wield the power that splits the earth and causes mountains to shake with every word, he chose to empty himself of that. Have you ever wondered why Jesus didn't do miracles that would have caused every person to believe in him, undeniable displays of the glory of God that would have been seen by every eye and heard by every ear? He chose not to! He chose not to call down fire on the abusive Roman soldiers as they tore the flesh from his back. Jesus needed people to believe that they could change the world, filled by the Spirit of God, as human beings. He chose to lay it all to one side to start a whole new race.

When you and I accepted the Jewish Rabbi Jesus as our Messiah, Lord and God we became part of another story, one that didn't start with Matthew, Mark, Luke and John but with a narrative of a God who has always looked to take a people out of a people, to display his power and love to a hurting world. We have been quarried out of the same rock as Abraham and Sarah. We are part of a family with roots that go deep into the sands of time, and have been invited to the family banquet, adopted as full sons and daughters.

 Throughout the Old Testament, the Bible tells of the people turning away from God, from the very beginning of their wanderings in the wilderness, through the leadership of Joshua, the judges and the kings. During his reign, Solomon began to heap up gold and silver and sell weapons to surrounding nations. When he sold chariots to his nation's neighbours, it was the equivalent of our selling tanks and bombs to those around us. He made political alliances through a ludicrous number of marriages – seven hundred wives and three hundred concubines! All these things were specifically prohibited in Deuteronomy 17:14–20, in which Solomon was instructed to write out a copy of the law, and to focus on these words every day of his life. This was intended to keep him from ending up in the mess that he eventually ended up in, but it seems he focused far more on the surrounding nations. God's heart was broken. The Hebrews were supposed to be different. The land was supposed to flow with milk and honey. They were supposed to be showing the world a new type of world, free of oppression, and yet here the rescued Hebrew slaves were becoming the ruthless slave masters. It was never meant to be this way!

The wild-eyed prophets began to cry out with

passion, trying to steer their people back to their divine purpose to be a light to the world. They were rejected time and time again, until the prophet Isaiah declared that as a result of the people's turning away from God they would be sent into exile (Isaiah 5:12–14). This is precisely what later occurred. However, God also promised that no matter what happened, he would always bring the Jews home and that his covenant with them would be an eternal one. This covenant promise has been fulfilled time and time again throughout history. When asked by Queen Victoria if he could provide proof that God exists, her Prime Minister Benjamin Disraeli (himself a Jew) thought for a moment and replied: 'The Jews, your Majesty'. God has always had a plan, and has always brought them home.

It has however, been a very rocky marriage. After years of flirting with foreign nations and the idols and religions they were bound to, the kingdom of Israel suffered a major attack was for the first time since it had become a sovereign nation under King David. Assyria destroyed the kingdom and tortured, killed and exiled many Jews. Later, in 586 BC, Babylon destroyed the southern kingdom of Judah. It too killed and exiled many Jews. In AD 135, the Romans killed an estimated 580,000 Jews and exiled many others. Finally, in AD 70 the Romans killed an estimated 1.1 million Jews and destroyed Jerusalem and the Temple.

For centuries Christendom persecuted the very

roots that we had been grafted into, committing awful atrocities that stain the pages of history with blood, and culminating in the horrific 'final solution' when, during the 1930s and 1940s, the Nazis, driven by evil, killed an estimated six million Jews.

Since then, millions of Jews worldwide have returned to their ancient homeland. Today, Israel again is a vibrant, independent country. But the empires of the Nazis, Romans, Babylonians and Assyrians have vanished. Today, we can judge with our own eyes as to whether Jeremiah was correct when he said, 2,600 years ago, that the enemies of the Jews would be destroyed, but that the Jews would be preserved. God is faithful and keeps his covenant.

God has given us the power and the promises to be people living in the way that Jesus lived and doing the things that he did. Our problem is that we have divorced ourselves from that area of Jesus' life where we can really see him as the flesh and blood man that he was in the context of the world in which he lived. 2 Peter 1:4 says: 'He has given us his very great and precious promises, so that through them you may participate in the divine nature and escape the corruption in the world caused by evil desires.' We would probably say something like: 'God has promised us amazing things so we are free to walk and talk and act like God.'

These are awesome words – if they weren't in the Bible they would sound blasphemous but they are right there and this is how God wants us to live. This poses an incredible, overwhelming challenge to humanity, because when Jesus says 'be like me', he means it. When he says, 'Follow me', he means it. He believes with every fibre of his being that you and I can be like him.

CHAPTER 2

THE EXODUS SEQUEL

The Babylonian empire was spectacular. The name in its original form meant 'The Gate of God', and it was commonly believed to have been founded by the rebel ruler Nimrod. The Hebrews used word play to change the name from Babili to Bilbel, from where we get the modern names Babel and Babylon, meaning 'confusion'. Despite the beauty and glory of this empire – its hanging gardens were known throughout the ancient world as an amazing wonder – this was not the gateway to God; it was a confusion built on the backs of slaves and cruel conquest. The empire reached its zenith at the time of Nebuchadnezzar II (604–561 BC) and at this time it dramatically intersects with the biblical narrative as Jerusalem is razed to the ground and the hopes of the Jewish nation seem to come to an abrupt end.

Exiles in the land held onto the hope that God would eventually bring them home, and God's children began to cry out to him again. The first exiles began to filter back after years of slavery and assimilation into Babylonian life and culture. We read in the book of Nehemiah that the children of Israel began to rebuild the Temple.

According to history these returning exiles were fiercely traditional – one might use the word 'conservative' in our day and age. They passionately believed in the scriptures and desired to follow those scriptures down to the 'jot and tittle'. Their God was the Yahweh of the Torah, and you only have to read the books of Nehemiah and Ezra to see how desperately they wanted to adhere to the words of God. Ezra 10:1 tells us that they found a scroll of the law – their hearts broke and everyone wept at the words and the recognition of their blatant failure to live up to God's commands. These returned exiles desperately wanted to make sure that they would never make the same mistake again in turning to worthless idols.

We tend to think that at this point everyone went home to the land of Israel. However, the reality was that vast numbers of Israelites decided to stay. In their reasoning there was no value in exchanging one form of slavery for another in a plundered, broken-down Israel, in need of rebuilding, heavily taxed by the empire and in danger from marauders and squatters. As a result they stayed in Babylon.

In 334 BC Alexander the Great conquered the Persian empire. One year later he attacked Israel and in the following year he took Jerusalem. The empire was then divided amongst his generals Seleucid (pronounced *Say-loo-chid*), Ptolemy, Antigonus and some others who were either killed or took smaller pieces of territory. Seleucid took Persia and parts of Asia Minor, and founded the Seleucid dynasty with Antioch as the capital city. Between 312 and 301 BC Antigonus I ruled Judah until he was killed at the Battle of the Kings. Israel then reverted to Seleucid rule.

The Seleucid dynasty had issues; it was marked by internal strife, which constantly drained and wore down the kingdom until it was taken by Tigranes of Armenia in 83 BC and annexed to the Roman empire by Pompey in 64 BC. Many lives were lost, blood spilt and battles fought. Within Israel itself though, there was another battle of far greater impact being fought – the battle for the mind. Not only had the land been invaded by a foreign power, but the very spiritual atmosphere had been encroached upon by a force that would shape the history of the world until our present day – Hellenism.

During Lent it has become a practice for me to fast from coffee. For me coffee is like a dear and close companion. It has seen me through difficult times and is a guilty pleasure. If I am out shopping with my wife or kids, a trip to the nearest and finest coffee watering hole will usually be first on my agenda. The deep hypnotic aroma of the sacred bean and the smooth silky taste of a full-bodied latte caresses all my senses, causing my spirit to rise and cry out, 'Yes, there is a God! How could anyone deny it?'

Twenty-five days or so into one Lent, my soul was longing for its coffee fix. I was on my way to conduct some training in micro-enterprise development and to teach in a youth retreat in the Amazon rainforest of Peru. Passing through the airport, I was confronted by the alluring aroma, then the soft jazz music and sofas – the mythical sea maiden in the logo was beckoning me to partake of a caramel macchiato. I just had to keep walking.

I made it past the temptation feeling pretty pleased with myself, but I could tell my travelling companion could see my struggle. We got through to the domestic terminal and wandered into the duty free shop to kill a bit of time. There before us was an array of free-to-try chocolate-covered coffee beans. There were plain chocolate beans, white chocolate beans, milk chocolate beans, coffee-flavoured chocolate beans – the enemy had pulled out the big guns! I turned to my companion, hoping for the green light – he just looked at me as if to say 'Dude, it's still coffee.'

To the side I noticed a refrigerator stacked up with ice cream made by the same company as the chocolate-covered coffee beans. It was coffee-flavoured ice cream! I turned to my friend and said, 'Come on, that must be OK, it's probably not even got real coffee in it.' We came to an agreement that if it had actual coffee extract then I would step away from the refrigerator – however, if it just said coffee flavouring then I would placate my craving. You guessed it – it was made from pure Peruvian coffee essence. Lent came and went and I'm glad to be able to say that I survived, just.

In reality it wasn't as difficult as I thought it would be. However, we all have incredibly strong longings, desires and cravings that, unfortunately, are not as easy to curb and control as simply leaving coffee for a while. We have an enemy who knows this all too well and is set on trying to tempt and get us off course.

The Hebrew word for Sin literally means to miss the target; it is taken from archery where the archer's intent is to send an arrow soaring from a bow at magnificent speed directly to the centre of the target, the bullseye. God as the great archer with precision and poise shoots us towards an incredible, breathtaking destiny but the adversary, the literal meaning of 'satan', is determined to intercept, to get us off course by any means possible, and his main strategy has not really changed since the very beginning.

When that sly serpent tempted the first humans in the Garden of Eden he did so in a very subtle and clever way in Genesis 3:1. First he challenged what they thought they knew. 'Did God really say...?' Adam and Eve were faced with a choice. Who or what was going to be the ultimate source of truth? Have you ever been there? 'God won't mind if I just ... will he? I mean, he is love, right? He made that juicy looking fruit ... it must be good.' God's command was, 'you must not eat from the tree...' (Genesis 2:16) and God never saw fit to explain to Adam and Eve why not. They were to accept it simply because God was God.

In spite of the almost complete freedom that God gives, they are about to stumble in the one command that he gives them. Not the 613 that would eventually be given to the children of Israel – just one. 'God knows you will be just like him' the serpent hisses. 'Just like him' was very tempting – they had seen Yahweh in all his glory, they walked and talked with him, they knew his power, and they had seen him creating universes. The great irony of course is that they already were like him – they were made in his image and clothed in his glory – but they wanted more. The temptation to see themselves as the ultimate authority in the world was overwhelming. They responded as the snake had hoped, and made themselves into their own god, crowned as the ultimate in the universe, free to determine their own actions and even God's. The stage was set. Hellenism was the logical result of this attitude.

The word 'Hellenism' itself originates from the Greeks (who were also known as Hellenes), and it is a set of beliefs that were advanced with religious ferocity by the empire. Although Alexander the Great is known primarily as a military commander, he claimed that his first objective and calling was as a missionary of Hellenism. It becomes complicated when we try to explain the basic tenets of Hellenism today as they were portrayed in Jesus' time: firstly, the empire absorbed all kinds of beliefs as it advanced, and secondly, throughout the following centuries and even to the present day Hellenism has intermingled with different thoughts and philosophies, from the humanism of modernity to the animism of the New Age.The word polytheism is derived from the Greek words poly ('many') and theos ('gods') and means 'worship of many gods'. The polytheism central to Hellenistic thought is therefore defined as a belief in the existence of many gods. It is the idea that divinity ultimately resides in many separate entities or beings. There were gods everywhere!

The most well-known of the Greek gods is Zeus – you probably instantly have a picture of a big, bearded guy, in a robe and carrying a lightning bolt. He was believed to be the god of the sky and ruler of the Olympian gods. In Roman mythology he was known as Jupiter. He was considered to be, according to Homer (not of *Simpsons* fame, but rather the ancient classical writer), the father of the gods and of all mortals. He was the big cheese, the head honcho! They didn't believe that Zeus created either gods or mortals, but he was their father, protector and ruler. He was thought to be the lord of the sky, the rain god, and the cloud gatherer, who wielded the terrible lightning bolt (the Canaanite god Baal, who we read of so often in the Hebrew scriptures, was also believed to control these elements). His breastplate was the aegis, his bird the eagle, his tree the oak.

However, despite its myriad of gods, Hellenism really worshipped self and self-realisation: the human form, human reason, passion and the senses, achievement and wealth. As such, Hercules was considered to be the ultimate symbol of the struggle of each mortal to make his or her way to Olympus, among the Immortal Ones. Hellenism worshipped both conscious forces of nature and also abstract ideas, such as harmony, justice, freedom, beauty, luck, lust, greed and so on. The Olympics were essentially a marketing event for Hellenism; they worshipped man and all his achievements. In Hellenism man truly made gods in his own image so he could worship his own, more often than not, depraved nature.

Many schools of thought made up Hellenism. There were Platonists, Aristotelians, Stoics and Epicureans, each espousing their own interpretation of the world around them. Some elements of these philosophies would later have a huge impact on Christianity in declaring the physical world to be transitory and evil and the spiritual world eternal

32

and good. Greek philosophy, particularly Plato's teaching on dualism, provided the background for the development of some of the extremes within the monastic movement, which encouraged the, at times, violent discipline of the body to 'free the spirit'. Greeks emphasised the rational mind, which created a tendency in Christianity to emphasise knowledge at the expense of obedience or experience.

The Greek educational system was highly effective, instilling Greek ideals into entire cultures. Statues of the Greek gods and heroes were placed everywhere and were clearly designed to celebrate the ultimate ideal, which was the human body. People read Homer, Euripides, and Plato and absorbed their man-centred values. The gymnasium (school), the theatre, the baths, the stadia and the Temples all presented Hellenism in all its implications and practices. The blossoming and expanding nature of culture, architecture, medicine and the latest technology were irresistible to many people.

Hellenism became the accepted way, and people began to see human wisdom as the greatest wisdom. Accomplishments in athletics, arts and architecture became the motivating drive. The human body was considered the ultimate in beauty so nudity in art, the baths, and sports was not only acceptable but encouraged and even flaunted. This in turn made the way for the fast growth of lust and worship of the created, rather than the creator. The Roman baths would later be known as glorified brothels and there is a wealth of documents describing the culture of orgies where excess was celebrated. From gorging on food and then paying a visit to the vomitorium, to multiple sexual partners, nothing was to be denied.

Accumulation of material things to provide luxury and comfort for one's self was considered a normal pursuit — charity and care for the less fortunate became almost nonexistent as the focus on I, me, and mine permeated the culture. To be the best, better than all others at any cost, was life's greatest goal.

The Greeks tried to build their society on gods who, though considered to be greater in power, were little different in character from the people who worshipped them. They were glorified humans, deities that the people created in their own image. In reality the foundation of their society, their worldview, came from their own imagination. They had nothing bigger than themselves on which to base their society, and though obviously there was much good within them and elements of their society, the overwhelming result was corruption. Their society would eventually collapse under its own decay.

Hellenism as a worldview is based on a belief that human beings are the ultimate source of truth and authority in the universe. This philosophy provided the foundation for a culture devoted to the supremacy of human beings and human accomplishment. We might look on such beliefs as foolish, but in reality we all fall into forms of idolatry. We still believe and worship the Hercules around us, the demigods striving to become the most successful, talented and beautiful. We see the struggle in the American Dream and the Hollywood hopefuls constantly striving for more, wealth, fame or power, or in the many religions and cults dedicated to improving Karma or following strict rituals. It is the self trying to reach God, rather than God reaching out to us. The lust for more drives us likes hamsters running in a wheel and we actually think that we are going somewhere. The illusion of power is enticing and this false belief that we can somehow be gods fuels the fire of violence and greed, whether in our streets or on the battle fields where war is raging right now.

Mahatma Gandhi said 'The day the power of love overrules the love of power, the world will know peace.' But that power of love can only come from outside us. 'God is love' said the Apostle John (1 John 4:8) – without him there is no real love and no real peace. It's no wonder that as Hellenism spread the known world became a horrifically violent place. US Army Field Commander Omar Bradley wisely noted in his memoirs, 'Ours is a world of nuclear giants and ethical infants. We know more about war than we know about peace, more about killing than we know about living. We have grasped the mystery of the atom and rejected the Sermon on the Mount.'

Today Hellenism has taken on a new face, in some ways a more honest face. It is called Humanism. Nevertheless, its worldview is the same. The glorification of human accomplishment, the drive to be number one, the obsession with comfort, pleasure and self, the focus on the human body and sexuality, the lack of compassion and sympathy for others, and the commitment to the will of the majority (of humans) as being right – all are built on the con that dates back to the Garden of Eden. The phrases that describe our culture could have come straight out of Asia Minor, where the gospel first reached. 'If it feels good, just do it ... because who can tell you that it is wrong for you?' Benjamin Franklin once said 'Many a man thinks he is buying pleasure, when he is really selling himself to it.'

In our day and age we think we are purchasing, when in reality we are being bought, enslaved. 'I deserve to have what I want,' we cry out. But hang on a minute – who can say what we really do or don't deserve? I for one am glad that I don't receive what I deserve! 'You have the right to do whatever you want with your body!' our culture defiantly declares. But since when is it 'my' body? Doesn't everything belong to God? And hasn't it all been given on loan as an amazing gift to enjoy and use to glorify him? The gymnasium of our world comes in many forms too, from our education system to huge influences in the arts, business and politics, and even tragically from thousands of pulpits every Sunday morning.

The battle that began that day in Eden continues. What will be the response of the people who know the truth and the lie? We live in the same world as the Jews of Jesus' day and the years leading up to his birth. Grasp this and you will grasp the radical nature of Jesus' life and message. The great task and mission of the believer is to live in a world where humanity is deemed supreme and to declare in life and example how false that view is. God alone is supreme.

CHAPTER 3

MAKING A MESSAGE OUT OF THE MESS

In the year 330 BC, the Jewish people were still putting together the pieces of a nation raped by empires that had risen and fallen. Now it was the Greeks' turn and Alexander marched in and conquered Judea. For the next two hundred years, the Jewish people become part of a Hellenistic kingdom. Much of Jewish aristocracy was attracted to the new way of thinking. Greek institutions like the gymnasium were founded in Jerusalem. Toleration of pagan Greek religious practices were now even encouraged.

However, many were not willing to bow the knee. They knew that everything about Hellenism was antithetical to their scriptures and way of life. Humans are not the ultimate in the universe, God is. Life is not to be lived for self but for him. The ultimate in beauty is God and through a relationship with him we can enjoy the beauty of all he has created. Truth is not what I happen to think and decide is best for me, but rather what God has revealed, is revealing, will reveal and what he allows his people to discover. Whether understood or not, his word is not questioned and heaven and earth will pass away, Olympus will pass away, but his word will not. The stage was set for a clash of kingdoms.

Now this was a land that was passionate for God, right? Their whole history and identity is centred around the fact that there is one true God,

> *Shema y'israel Adonai eloheinu.*
> Hear O Israel, the Lord is one.

This was their God and this God had made stipulations as to what was expected and commandments that he has given us the free will to choose if we want to walk in the amazing blessings that he has promised us. It was only a matter of time before the clashes would come.

By now Israel was filling up again with returned refugees, pockets of dissidents, rebels and misfits. Samaritans, a race of mixed tribes mingled with Jews to form what the Rabbis would later term a 'mongrel race', became alienated from the rest of the Jews and were forced to set up a rival faith. Traditionalists and syncretists were spouting off different ideas and worldviews. Hellenists were prostituting their civilisation to any who would pay the price and get in bed with the latest fads. The Romans were raping and stealing whatever they could for the so-called *pax romana*, peace at the cost of hundreds of crucified dissidents. Zealot freedom fighters were bleeding the land, hoping that the blood of Abel crying out for justice would excuse their violence. The land was groaning and waiting for something else – waiting for the sons of God to come into their fullness – and on it goes year in, year out.

Into this volatile atmosphere came a rural Jewish priest from Modin. His name was Mattathias the Hasmonean. He was outraged by the Greek decree outlawing Jewish religious practice and the desecration of the Jewish Temple by the ruler Antiochus Epiphanes, who had placed Greek idols in the Temple, entered the Holy of Holies and sacrificed pigs on the great altar, spreading their blood amongst the Temple grounds. His son Judas Maccabeus led a small army in guerrilla warfare against the Seleucids, finally claiming back Jerusalem. Israel was once again a free nation.

The Jewish festival of Hanukkah celebrates the re-dedication of the Temple to Yahweh, and according to Rabbis the story goes that Judas could only find a small jug of the sacred oil that burnt in the fire of the great menorah candle that had not been contaminated. Although there was only sufficient oil for one day, God miraculously caused the oil to burn for eight days. Finally the land was free again, though it would not be so for long, and the hundreds of thousands who had stayed in Babylon decided that it was now time to make their way home.

When the people returned from Babylon following the Maccabee revolt they settled in the area of Galilee, mainly because it was largely unpopulated, and huge numbers returned at this point. In stark contrast to the earlier returned exiles, these guys were not traditionalists. They had spent centuries hoping and believing in the fiery messages of the prophets and waiting expectantly in Babylon for the revolution and restoration of Israel. They were, as they now saw it, finally seeing God revive the people. Their theology was founded on prophecy, signs and wonders. They believed in the angelic preservation of Shadrach, Meshach and Abednego, and in Daniel and Ezekiel's prophetic encounters of the heavens. They longed to see the healing power of Elijah and Elisha in the face of the false claims of idols. They were the supernaturals, those that would raise their hands, sing and dance; some sources talk of the Hasidim trembling under the power of the Holy Spirit.

As far as the Judeans were considered these guys were just plain weird – they were the crazy charismatics. Though in distance Galilee and Judea were so close, theologically they might as well have been from opposite sides of the world. 'Your Yahweh is not my Yahweh', said the Sadducee to the Pharisee. 'Your interpretation of Torah is not my interpretation of Torah', the Pharisee would respond. This was not unlike our modern day squabbles, pitching our personal views of Jesus against one another or dogmatically holding to our interpretation alone.

As far as the traditionalists were concerned, at the time of the Babylonian exile the 'canon' closed. There was no more healing, no more prophecy, no more need for God to speak in the same way. After all, they reasoned, we now have the glorious Temple and the rituals, why would we need God to say anything else. Sound familiar? The cessationist theology of today would argue that signs and wonders and prophecy is no longer needed in the body of Christ because we have the scriptures. The word (print on paper) of God ends up being worshipped over the God of the word who still breathes truth into the soul of anyone willing to receive it.

41

The Hasmonean dynasty, descendants of the once radical Judas Maccabee, proved to be the perfect mixing bowl for all kinds of different religious groups to spring up. This was the dramatic backdrop to the stage on which Jesus would play out his ministry, This was the mess from which a new and awesome message would soon break forth.

Maria spent the day wearing her daughter's picture in a small pendant hanging from her neck, like a precious jewel on a necklace. It was the only way that she could hold her daughter close to her heart. Ana was gone; all that was left was this picture in a pendant still sparkling in the Andean sunshine.

Ana had wanted to be a doctor, and she was well on her way to seeing her dream fulfilled. Despite amazing odds set against her, she had that feisty, winning attitude that I have seen time and time again in the nation of Colombia, a nation that has been ravaged by decades of pain and suffering and yet is full of people who can still hold their heads up high and smile with a warmth and affection that is contagious. The armed conflict between the Colombian government and guerrilla movements such as the Revolutionary Armed Forces of Colombia (FARC), and the National Liberation Army (ELN) has existed since around 1964. It has its roots in the conflict known as La Violencia, which was triggered by the 1948 assassination of the much admired political leader Jorge Eliecer Gaitan, and also in the aftermath of US-backed military attacks on poor communities in rural Colombia in the 1960s. This led both liberal and communist militants to re-organise into the so-called Revolutionary Armed Forces of Colombia.

Ana left her home in a rural area of Colombia to attend medical school, and after she finished, returned to provide care for members of her community. Her community was just one of a myriad in which tens of millions of Colombians live on less than two dollars a day. The bullies and cowards of this world always look for those that they can assume a false sense of power over and Ana's vulnerable community was no exception. At the hands of left-wing guerrilla fighters, right-wing paramilitaries and even members of the military they were subject to physical and sexual abuse from powerful weaklings whose cowardice hid behind their swagger, leaving debris in the wake of their greed.

The reasons for fighting vary hugely from group to group. The FARC and other guerrilla movements claim to be fighting for the rights of the poor in Colombia to protect them from government violence and to provide social justice based on a Marxist understanding of socialism. It is therefore, a glaring hypocrisy every time we hear stories of yet another family or community displaced, a farm robbed, an innocent life taken. The Colombian government on the other hand, claims to be fighting for order and stability, and seeking to protect the rights and interests of its citizens. The paramilitary groups, forged in the fires of desire for revenge, saw that the Colombian system failed to provide them with justice, so they took matters into their own hands. Over the course of time groups such as the AUC (United Armed Forces of Colombia), emerged, claiming to be reacting to perceived threats by the guerrilla movements. To quote the Prince of Verona in Shakespeare's Romeo and Juliet, in this story 'all are punished.' There are no winners, just blood-stained ground and territory gripped in white-knuckled rage and the fear that tomorrow it could be snatched away. Both guerrilla and paramilitary groups have been found drug trafficking to fuel their fight for a 'utopia', and everyone involved has bowed the knee to terror tactics. All parties engaged in the conflict, including state forces, have been criticised for numerous human rights violations. The fighting has killed tens of thousands of people, and displaced millions. It has made Colombia the nation with the second highest level of displaced people in the world after Sudan.

Despite Ana's vulnerable position, she would not keep quiet. Deep in our gut, in the core of who we are something cries out for justice – we are made in the image of a God who weeps with us, who lifts up the downtrodden, who comes alongside the abused. This is why the fire burns in the essence of who we are to see a better tomorrow than yesterday, a new world burst forth in the shell of the old. She travelled around Colombia to voice her concerns. It was not made any easier when Ana became pregnant. Despite the human rights abuses by paramilitaries, the military, and the insurgency groups, Ana continued to speak out until she met the abuses she was fighting first hand at a rebel checkpoint.

Maria recounted the event from her investigation. Pregnant Ana was pulled from a car and raped by the soldiers. A knife was plunged into her stomach and her unborn baby was removed and killed. What followed is too gruesome to recount, but is simply one of the overwhelming number of horror stories told in a nation reeling in pain. And why is this so? Because people have just as much capacity to hate as to love, to find differences rather than to look for the common beautiful thread of divine DNA that runs at the core of us all. Why have Catholics and Protestants, Arabs and Jews, socialists and fascists, The Rolling Stones and The Beatles, and everyone in between fought, sometimes for centuries? As in the prologue for those star crossed-lovers Romeo and Juliet, there are many feuds in which the roots are buried so deep under the mists of time that we are no longer even clear on where it all started. This can certainly be seen in the saga that caused tensions to rise and blood to boil in first-century Judea and Samaria.

Jesus was asked by an, 'expert in the law' on one occasion what he must do to inherit eternal life. He wasn't asking how to get into heaven, but rather how to live in the centre of God's great story, life bubbling forth in abundance here and now. Essentially he was saying 'What do I have to do to get this life right?' Have you ever thought to yourself, 'If I just knew the most important thing, the essence, everything would be OK? If I could just drown out the static and the noise long enough to have concentrated focus on what really matters, then imagine what could be achieved? Imagine what life could be.'

In Luke 10:26–28 Jesus replies to the expert on the law:

'What is written in the Law?' [Jesus] replied. 'How do you read it?' He answered, 'Love the Lord your God with all your heart and with all your soul and with all your strength and with all your mind'; and, 'Love your neighbour as yourself.'

In the Second Temple Period it is fair to say that this was one of the central discussion points. If Torah is the centre of our faith and to live by Torah is to walk with

45

the divine and to be soaring like an arrow shot from his bow, directly towards that centre, that destiny that Yahweh has planned, then it is of utmost importance to get it right. The problem was that this was easier said than done. Through interpretations passed down by oral tradition through the ages it was estimated that there were 613 commands and some seemed to directly contradict each other. 'I'm not to work on Sabbath, but I'm commanded to rescue, even if, like we read in the scripture, it's a donkey fallen into a pit. The exertion would be considered work so what am I to do?' Were some commandments more important than others, or to use the Rabbinic terminology, 'lighter' and 'weightier'? If so, who was to say which was more important? Could anyone be so presumptuous as to categorise the divine utterances? How can we know?

Every Rabbi had their way of interpreting the scriptures, known as their 'yoke'. People wanting to follow the Rabbi would test their yoke. This is what is happening in this exchange between the teacher of the law and Jesus. We need to reassess what we have been taught about these exchanges in the scriptures, because I am almost certain that at some point you will have either consciously or unconsciously thought that whenever they take place the questioner is trying to trick Jesus. There are occasions when that is true, but often what is actually happening is an honest search for truth under the assumption that, just maybe, Jesus is who he says he is. To test a Rabbi's yoke was a sign of great respect, and in most cases it showed a desire to follow that particular Rabbi. So look at this exchange with the fresh eyes of a devoted, committed follower of Yahweh in search of the truth. Jesus is more than happy to enter into the dialogue to compliment the man's wisdom and to take him into a deeper revelation:

'You have answered correctly,' Jesus replied. 'Do this and you will live.' But he wanted to justify himself, so he asked Jesus, 'And who is my neighbour?'

Luke 10:28–29

His desire to 'justify' himself isn't some pompous posturing but rather a desire to go deeper – he is essentially saying, 'Jesus, I do realise that to be the most important, but I need clarity.' This was a perfectly reasonable question because even the Hebrew word for neighbour holds ambiguities and certain nuances making it difficult to give a concrete answer. The Greek word is *plesion* and corresponds to the Hebrew word *re'a:* both can be rendered to mean a friend, companion, fellow, another person, an intimate friend, any other person 'nearby', and where two are concerned. Coupled with this difficulty is the fact that the main schools of thought from Rabbi Shammai and Rabbi Hillel on who your 'neighbour' was were very different. At the time of Jesus, according to many the term *re'a* was exclusively used for any member of the Hebrew nation and commonwealth. It is clear that Jesus decides it is time for this word and concept to get a revolutionary makeover:

In reply Jesus said: 'A man was going down from Jerusalem to Jericho, when he was attacked by robbers. They stripped him of his clothes, beat him and went away, leaving him half dead. A priest happened to

47

be going down the same road, and when he saw the man, he passed by on the other side. So too, a Levite, when he came to the place and saw him, passed by on the other side. But a Samaritan, as he travelled, came where the man was; and when he saw him, he took pity on him. He went to him and bandaged his wounds, pouring on oil and wine. Then he put the man on his own donkey, brought him to an inn and took care of him. The next day he took out two denarii and gave them to the innkeeper. 'Look after him,' he said, 'and when I return, I will reimburse you for any extra expense you may have.'

'Which of these three do you think was a neighbour to the man who fell into the hands of robbers?'

The expert in the law replied, 'The one who had mercy on him.'

Jesus told him, 'Go and do likewise.'

Luke 10:30:37

We know the story – it's probably one of the earliest we learnt in Sunday school or nursery and the common understanding goes that it's all about doing good to your neighbour. A good Samaritan is someone who helps someone in need, right? That's what Jesus is saying to do, isn't he?

There's a large charity in the UK known as 'The Samaritans' and it is essentially a service offering care and support to people in desperation by providing a caring listening ear. The idea isn't to counsel, to offer answers, to sort out the person's problem, but simply to listen. In my job as a church leader I can't begin to tell you how many times someone has asked to come and speak to my wife and I and have shared their hearts and cried their tears only to come to the answer all by themselves, without us having to say a word. This is always encouraging for me as quite honestly, we usually don't have the answer anyway! They just needed someone to listen to them. The world is desperately in need of people to help and love people in need, to bandage up their wounds and ensure that they will be taken care of.

However, that is not what this story is about. It's not even close. If we want to understand the radical, subversive nature of Jesus' stories and parables we must understand them in their original Jewish context. Jesus' audience, hearing this story for the first time, would have stood in shock and amazement that Jesus would even dare to suggest such a thing! They had reason to feel this way.

The Samaritans lived in the north/south divide between the traditionalist Judeans to the south and the nonconformist, more charismatic Galileans to the north, in the barren land of Samaria or *Shechem*. Because of their defective devotion to Judaism and their partly pagan ancestry, the Samaritans were despised by ordinary Jews. Because the Samaritans were sometimes hostile, and also because Jews believed that they could become contaminated by passing through Samaritan territory, Jews who were travelling from Judea to Galilee or vice versa would cross over the Jordan river and avoid Samaria by going through Transjordan, and cross back over the river again once they neared their destination.

The Samaritans often taunted the Jews. They rejected all of the Old Testament except the Torah, and to rub a bit of salt in the wound, they claimed to have an older copy than the Jews and boasted that they observed the precepts correctly and with greater dedication. The Jews despised them for it and repaid them with hatred. They rejected the Samaritan copy of the Torah and publicly denied that Samaritans had any Jewish birthright – they were illegitimate, outcast, mongrels. To the Jews they were worse than animals; they were not made in the image of God (John 4:12). Samaritans were publicly cursed in their synagogues, could not serve as witnesses in the Jewish courts, could not be converted to Judaism as proselytes and were excluded from the afterlife.

Excuse me? Excluded from the afterlife? Really? And who exactly made that decision? What was the big deal? Why couldn't they just get on with each other? For that we need to go back quite some time and as with all feuds, we will find that the roots that seem so petty and small went incredibly deep.

 It is impossible to write an accurate history of the Samaritans because their records are so scarce, and their references are often contradictory. First of all the name 'Samaritan' only appears once in the Old Testament, in 2 Kings 17:29, where it is used for the colonist newcomers, planted by the Assyrians, who, according to the scriptures, persisted in their pagan ways. However, the majority of the population consisted of Israelites who had not been deported and who continued in their Israelite faith. The beliefs brought by the newcomers did not survive and no paganism is found in later Samaritan theology. On the contrary, they seem to have been more fiercely devoted to the Torah, albeit their own interpretation of it, than any of the other groups in Jesus' day.

The mixed population of Samaria was not accepted as Jewish by the Jews of the south, that is in Judea. When the Jews returned from the Babylonian exile and began to rebuild the Temple, the Samaritans offered to help, and perhaps here we see one of those moments in history where so much pain could have been averted. Accepting the Samaritans' help could have brought life, restoration and reconciliation; unfortunately the Jews chose conflict and division and the Samaritans' offer was rejected. In their bitterness over this decision they then proceeded to prevent or delay the project (Ezra 4:1–6).

Jesus' disciples one day stopped a man who was healing in Jesus' name, saying that he 'wasn't one of us'. Jesus rebuked them, saying that if someone is not against the advancement of his kingdom, then they can be used for and by him. How many out there are bringing healing, fighting injustice, loving the unlovely and showing mercy in the name of love? Maybe they are not part of our group, maybe they don't wear the same clothes, listen to the same music or hold the same doctrine, but they are, whether consciously or not, advancing Jesus' movement on the earth. They may not even realise that it's his movement, or that they are following his agenda, but nonetheless they are unwittingly doing God's business. The Jews lost the Samaritans because they chose to drive a wedge between them, to build a wall instead of working together.

When the returned exiles began to rebuild the walls of Jerusalem, the Samaritans protested to the king of Persia that this constituted an act of rebellion and high treason, and the work was stopped until the arrival of Nehemiah, who King Artaxerxes commissioned as governor (Ezra 4:7–24). The Samaritans maintained their hostile attitudes and actions, which were now directed with increasing venom against Nehemiah (Nehemiah 6:1–13). Their opposition was not successful, but that didn't stop the growing animosity between each group from reaching boiling point. The division was now complete. Samaritans were forbidden to offer sacrifices at the Temple in Jerusalem or to intermarry with Jews, while in retaliation and competition the Samaritans built their own Temple on Mount Gerazim, near Shechem. Their Bible consisted of the Torah alone; the text features small changes from the accepted Hebrew text and also contains additional verses specifically mentioning Mount Gerazim as the site of the Temple.

In the following centuries, the Samaritans suffered when Shechem was destroyed by Alexander the Great, while in 128 BC John Hyrcanus captured Shechem and destroyed the Samaritan Temple. It remained in ruins until the second century AD, when it was rebuilt by the Emperor Hadrian as a reward for the help he received from the Samaritans against the Jews during the Bar Kokhba revolt (AD 132–135).

The ongoing hostility between Jews and Samaritans pops up time and time again in the

New Testament. One of the worst insults that hostile listeners could, like petulant children, hurl at Jesus, was to call him a Samaritan! (John 8:48). When Jesus was refused hospitality by a Samaritan village because he had 'set his face' to go to Jerusalem, his disciples James and John were so enraged that they wanted to call fire down on them and totally annihilate them. It seems the disciples still had a lot to learn! (Luke 9:51–56)

If you were a Jew walking through a predominantly Samaritan area you were likely to get your throat cut. Likewise if you were a Samaritan walking through a predominantly Jewish area it could be your last journey. It is well documented in the Talmud that Rabbi Shammai, considered one of the greatest Rabbis, alongside Rabbi Hillel was once asked:

'Rabbi Shammai, what is the greatest command?'
    'Love the Lord your God with all your mind, heart and strength and love your neighbour as yourself' replied Shammai.
    'And who is my neighbour? Must I love the Babylonian? Is he my neighbour?'
    'Yes of course, he is made in the image of God.'
    'What about the Greek? Is the Greek my neighbour?'
    'Yes of course, he too is made in the image of God.'
    'And Rabbi Shammai, what about the Roman, surely not the Roman?'
    'Yes even the Roman is made in the image of God, he too is your neighbour.'

'Rabbi Shammai, what about the Samaritan?'

'No! Never the Samaritan! My son, the Samaritan is not made in the image of God!'

In this context we start to comprehend just how revolutionary Jesus' conversation with the Samaritan woman at the well in John chapter 4 really was. A Samaritan! Good? A 'good' Samaritan? Inconceivable! And yet this is the brilliance of Jesus – time and time again in the parables, he draws his audience in, lulls them into a sense of false security by using the usual template parable formats and then socks it to them when they least expect it. Jesus uses a sequence that we see in the Mishnah whereby a Rabbi would tell a parable featuring a Levite, a priest, and then a Pharisee, a bit like our Englishman, Irishman, Scotsman joke formats. His crowd thought they knew what was coming.

First, along comes a priest, one of the Sadducees. They were very strict in their observance of Torah and the laws of Moses, with a strong bias toward anything that pertained to the Temple and sacrificial system. Following hot on the priest's trail comes a Levite, who is also a Sadducee. As such he is obliged to follow Torah to the letter of the law. This is important because they both consider this obligation as of greater importance than their obligation to preserve life. Jesus uses dry humour when he says they passed by on the 'other side of the road' – these roads were very narrow and there was no 'other side'. They had to confront the reality of the suffering in front of them. The same is true for us today. We can't change the channel and pretend that makes us exempt from doing something about the suffering we've just seen. It's in front of us, right there, on our journey, bleeding, hurting, half dead, desperately needing someone to do something. We must not cross over the road and hurry off on our way.

The subtle term in Jesus' parable, 'leaving him half dead', is very important. An argument raged in Jesus' day with regards to these laws and what God really intended with these guidelines. The Hebrew term is *goses,* and according to the teachings of the Pharisees if someone was in this state it was imperative that one did everything within one's power to help the person. Even if this poor, unfortunate man had died, there was a *met mitzvah* or command/duty to bury the dead. Life was to come first and the Rabbis coined the phrase *Pikuach Nefesh* ('Life comes first') to state this. It meant that any law or commandment could be suspended if a life was at stake.

Hillel claimed that it didn't matter if you were the high priest on the Day of Yom Kippur, if you could save a life that was more important than anything else. Life must be preserved above your strict adherence to the law. This was for the most part, accepted as a reasonable expectation, so while Jesus' audience may not have been hugely surprised that the Sadducees in Jesus' cast of players responded in this way, they would certainly have been disappointed in them.

I believe that at this point Jesus' audience thought they knew exactly what was coming next. They thought to themselves, 'Ha, Jesus is going to show, those, pompous, stuck-up Sadducees – he's going to have a godly, respected Pharisee show up now and do the right thing!' So imagine their shock and horror when Jesus says that the next person to show up is a Samaritan!

The man has been stripped of his clothes, beaten and

left half dead. This is important for a number of reasons. Firstly Samaritans and Jews dressed and spoke differently, but being left 'half dead' meant the man wasn't going to be giving any speeches, so everything that identified this man was gone. He was vulnerable, without covering, naked, transparent. We all have our colours, our symbols, our styles and terminology. We want to belong, but the flipside of that is segregation and alienation from those that aren't part of our tribe. Underneath it all we're skin and bones. We're made of the same substance – cut any of us and we bleed. We are all made in the image of God and so we are all neighbours. The Samaritan comes and reverses what has been inflicted on this unfortunate traveller. The man is stripped, beaten, left half dead, then we read that the Samaritan bandages the wounds, pours on oil and makes sure that he is taken care of. We are called to reverse the pain we see around us, to turn things around, to restore, rebuild and renew.

Now here is the power punch in Jesus' story. The Samaritan, just like the Levite and priest, adhered with dogged tenacity to the Torah. He wanted to live to the letter the teachings of Moses. However he was willing to lay his theology down, to lay his culture down, to lay his prejudice down to save and preserve life, even if that was for his most hated enemy. He would see him, with everything stripped away, made in the image of God. Love is greater than our differences.

Who is our neighbour? According to Jesus, our worst enemy is our neighbour! Let me soften the blow, because we don't like to think we hate anyone. But who do you find it impossible to love? Maybe someone did you great wrong. Maybe you can't even picture them without those memories flooding back and stinging you again. Maybe someone separated your family, took someone you love deeply from you. Maybe someone abused you terribly. Jesus says they are your neighbour, made in the image of God and you must love them. Impossible? Absolutely. That is why we need Jesus.

Loving your neighbour, it turns out, is nowhere near as easy as it sounds. Living this out at the level that Jesus is talking about requires something more. It requires the indwelling power of the Holy Spirit, transforming us and causing God's subversive, insurgent, counterintuitive love to swell in our hearts. Jesus shows us that it is possible too, as hanging on a cross, his blood drips into the sand and with the life ebbing away from his body he says, 'Forgive them, for they do not know what they are doing'.

There are Samaritans all around us. We are Samaritans to many around us. We fight and hate and divide and scheme. We gather and congregate and join forces and attack. Often we don't even know why, how, when or where the feud began. At other times we know exactly where our hate stems from. Jesus is saying if we want to live in the 'age to come' to 'inherit eternal life', to see heaven on earth, we must, must, love our neighbours as ourselves.

One can only imagine how different things could have been if there had been an atmosphere of inclusion and hope right at the beginning of this great divorce. Could it have been that God's love would have led those early Samaritans into a right relationship with him? Instead, due to their Hebrew brothers excluding them, they were forced to form their own rival faith.

For the sake of all the Anas and their unborn children we must heed Jesus' command to 'Go and do likewise'; we must learn from the mistakes of the past. To truly be followers of Jesus, walking in the dust of our Rabbi, the one known as a 'friend of sinners and outcasts', we would do well to invite the New-Ager, homosexual, Hindu, Buddhist, Jehovah's Witness, Scientologist, transsexual and anyone else made in the image of God, from whatever walk of life, around the world, with views different and even diametrically opposed to ours, to the party that is God's kingdom on earth and to show the love of Jesus in all its awesome transforming power.

CHAPTER 4

MASKED MISFITS:
THE SADDUCEES

There was a Rabbi, a Hindu Brahman priest and a televangelist who all happened to be travelling and, as chance would have it, they arrived together at a country hotel at the same time. There was, however, a problem – the hotel only had two rooms. The owner cautiously suggested the stable: 'It's not much, but it will keep you warm and there are no other hotels for miles around.' All being 'holy men' they wanted to put the other first and so the Rabbi was quick to say 'I'll stay in the stable.' A short time later, however, he came back and knocked on the door. 'I'm afraid I can't stay in the stable – you see, there is a pig in there and as you know we consider pigs as un-kosher and unclean. I'm afraid I cannot stay out there.' The Hindu priest perked up: 'Please don't concern yourself – I am very happy to stay in the stable.' But after a matter of minutes, there was another knock on the door as the Hindu priest returned shaking his head. 'I am very, very sorry but I also cannot stay in the stable – you see, there is

*a cow in there with the pig and the cow is considered sacred
in our religion. I am not permitted to sleep in your stable.'
The televangelist looked around to see if there were any other
options, and realising there were none begrudgingly replied:
'OK, I suppose I can stay in the stable.' The televangelist had
not been long gone, when once again, the now exasperated
inn keeper heard a knock on the door. On opening the door
there before him stood the pig and the cow with a look of
desperation on their faces as if to say, 'Please don't make us
stay in there with the televangelist!'*

We've all seen them, in slick tailored suits and even slicker hairstyles, like travelling salesmen thrust upon a large stage with lizardly lithe words, selling Jesus, selling healing, selling salvation, all with a simple call to a toll-free line where all you will need to do is give your credit card details and all your troubles will miraculously disappear. Don't get me wrong, there are many great and humble men and women of God who build up and train the body of Christ and advance the kingdom in all kinds of ways using television as a platform and I am not out to knock them – many are wonderful people and I have had the privilege of being able to meet some and call others close friends. No, rather I am talking about those who use their stage and platform for personal gain and have little regard for the cause of Christ but great regard for the cause of cash!

Unless you have had your head buried in the sand since the beginning of the twenty-first century, you will have become sick, tired and even numb to the repeated scandals that continue to break in the news. Pastors caught with prostitutes; others faking life-threatening illnesses to get their 'testimony' bigged up; revivalists burnt out by a different fire than that of the Holy Spirit and looking for an outlet through adultery. It is by no means limited to the evangelical world – we are constantly bombarded by stories of yet another Catholic priest's impropriety. Then there are the stories that have hit us in the business world. On 2 December 2001, Enron filed for bankruptcy under chapter 11 of the US Bankruptcy Code. Approximately 63.4 billion dollars in assets were stolen or lost in the system, making it the largest corporate bankruptcy in history until WorldCom's bankruptcy the following year. Many executives at Enron were indicted for a variety of charges and were later given prison sentences.

If we are not careful it is very easy to get cynical and critical, but in the moments of brutal honesty with ourselves we know that but for the grace of God, we could find ourselves in the same position. However I think what really riles us the most is that even when perpetrators are caught red-handed, the lies and excuses continue to flow. In God's economy the repentant heart is always received with arms open wide, and there are always a thousand second chances when we pick ourselves up, dust ourselves off and run back to our Father's house. What's not so easy to square are the masks, lies and deceit that we can so easily choose to live behind.

It has been noted that the simplest, most basic, though highly flawed level of leadership and influence is based on position, nothing more. This is the type of leadership where people obey and follow you, for no other reason than your title, position or uniform. In Nazi Germany a soldier with a swastika emblazoned on his arm could order someone around and offer horrific retribution should they even consider disobeying. You may have the most arrogant, banal boss in the history of humanity, yet you have to obey them. Why? Because of their position and the authority it awards them. This level of leadership only produces grudging followers who have little other option. They do what they do because they have to.

This was the world and leadership of the Sadducees – they were slick salesmen, traffickers of Temple trinkets, masked misfits robed and uniformed to hide the truth. Sadducees, or Tzodokis, claimed to be the descendants of the high priest Zadok who officiated in the Temple during the days of King David and then King Solomon.

In 63 BC the Romans, after much fighting, finally broke the Jewish resistance and once again Israel was under the yoke of foreign power. The Romans were not about to put up with a Hasmonean dynasty that spoke of so much national pride and history fermenting like yeast within this newly acquired batch of dough. Even in AD 37 , when they were all but wiped out following Mark Antony's installation of the Idumean Herod as King, Herod still felt the need to marry the Hasmonean princess Mariamne to make his position 'kosher'. One of the interesting things to note is the manner by which the Romans began to draw them into their world – it was sly and potent and most importantly, it worked. Rather than using the sword they were able to pull the Hasmoneans off course using the temptations of the new world. It is much easier to con someone into thinking that you are their friend, than to live life as enemies.

Historians argue on the exact details of the transition

but somehow many of the Hasmoneans and their followers made their way into the sect of the Sadducees and began to take a more and more influential role. During the Hasmonean period, the Sadducees and Pharisees functioned primarily as political parties. Although the Pharisees had opposed the wars of expansion of the Hasmoneans and the forced conversions of the Idumeans, the political rift between them became wider when Pharisees demanded that the Hasmonean king Alexander Jannaeus choose between being king and being High Priest. In response, the king openly sided with the Sadducees by adopting their rites in the Temple. His actions caused a riot in the Temple and led to a brief civil war that ended with a bloody repression of the Pharisees, although at his deathbed the king called for reconciliation between the two parties. But the Sadducees' Temple and state relationship was by now tightly set and much blood would be shed in the coming civil wars before the Roman occupation. The Sadducees and Pharisees would be sworn enemies until the destruction of the Temple.

What did all of this mean to the Levitical priesthood of the Sadducees? Clearly the law was being deeply compromised on many levels. Hasmoneans and others bribed their way in and began to officiate in all kinds of different spheres revolving around the Temple worship in Jerusalem, bringing unheard-of corruption, especially when the ever-paranoid Herod began to pour in the gold from his coffers to create what he had determined would be the greatest Temple the ancient world had ever seen. The Sadducees soon became one of history's interesting paradoxes. On the one hand they demanded adherence to the law, in the ways that it related to the Temple and in as much as it benefited them and filled their pockets. On the other hand they seemed intent on living like the Hellenistic world around them, enjoying everything Rome had to offer. Many Sadducean homes have been found with Roman mosaics displaying and glorifying Roman mythology; Sadducees were known to attend the theatres and participate in the vices of the Roman baths. They were very wealthy, extorting large sums of money from the people through a monopoly on being able to declare which animals were pure enough to be sacrificed and which weren't.

The Indian poet and playwright Rabindranath Tagore stated: 'Your mission is proving that a love for the earth, and for the things of the earth, is possible without materialism, a love without greed ... I entreat you not to be turned by the call of vulgar strength, of stupendous size, by the spirit of storage.' The Sadducees were the materialists of their day and it had made them spiritually fat and lazy, apathetic towards the world around them. They were hypnotised by the vulgar strength of power, albeit false power under the Romans' ever-watching gaze. The stupendous size and magnificence of the Temple was in reality far more a palace to their own achievements and pride – the spirit of storage, always wanting more and never being satisfied.

We see Jesus at his most 'ticked off' because of the mafia-like control that Annas exerted in the sale of animals for sacrifice, in what historians believe was the court of the Gentiles. Not only were the priests taking what little money many of the poorer worshippers had, but they were also stopping the Gentiles from coming to the one true God. No wonder Jesus was so angry!

Sadly, the spirit of the Sadducees lives on among us, even in our own skin from time to time if we are brutally honest with ourselves. We see it displayed in an extreme way when the church 'sanctuary' is turned into something palatial and idolised above the God who declared, 'Heaven is my throne, and the earth is my footstool. Where is the house you will build for me?' (Isaiah 66:1); where hurting people are encouraged to purchase their miracle by dialling the number at the bottom of the screen and giving their card details. The Sadducee wears a mask, a mask that looks respectable but hides a heart that is black as tar. One of the greatest dangers as we battle the Sadducee within and the Sadducee spirit in the church is that it looks so good and respectable and can very easily deceive us into thinking we are fighting for God, like the crowd of Sadducees who cried out 'Crucify him!', when all the while Jesus weeps at our actions.

It was the Sadducees who pushed for the arrest, the illegal trial and the crucifixion of Jesus. Their call for Jesus' crucifixion was due to their shrewd awareness that this Nazarene revolutionary was causing the most powerful stir since Judas Maccabeus had stood up and said 'no more'. Their great fear was not that Jesus was teaching something new and different – there were plenty of radicals doing that in the different Rabbinic schools and amongst the various sects dotted around the Judean, Samaritan and Galilean landscape. It was that they knew that the hearts of the people had turned to Jesus and their position of privilege and their income was at great risk. Jesus was killed for the same reason that most modern day revolutionaries are taken out – politics. The kings of corruption and religious rule let fear drive them insane with jealousy as they watched this humble Rabbi inspire the hearts of the people they had controlled for so long.

The central figure and head of the Sadducees was the high priest Caiaphas, also known as Yosef Bar Kayafa. He was the son-in-law of the highly respected and ruthless high priest Annas, and would be the high priest who ruled longer than any other during New Testament times. His actual time in this position lasted between AD 18–36 . He was somewhat of a puppet ruler according to extra-biblical references, bowing to the commands of his father-in-law Annas. Before Caiaphas no less than four of Annas' sons had held the same office, following their father's mafia-like order. Annas was the first high priest of the newly formed Roman province of Judea in AD 6. He was ruthless to the core and was finally deposed by the procurator Gratus 'for imposing and executing capital sentences which had been forbidden by the imperial government'. Needless to say Caiaphas was always in his father-in-law's shadow.

To give him his due it was a very difficult time for Jewish leaders: there were serious concerns about the despotic rule of the Roman empire, but the terrorist threat of the insurgent Zealot movement aiming to eject the Romans from Israel also directly

66

challenged them. Both were encroaching, powerful pressures, weighing down on their precarious, protective bubble of power. Caiaphas controlled the Sanhedrin Jewish council, which comprised a 70 per cent majority of Sadducees, with the remaining 30 per cent made up of Pharisees, mainly of the school of Shammai. These were the more orthodox and conservative of the Pharisees, holding to the letter of the law.

In Matthew 21:12–17 we find the account of Jesus going into the Temple courts and overturning the tables of the money changers. Annas owned and controlled all the booths here, so Jesus' actions alone were a direct attack on Annas' power; however, Jesus made an even more pointed criticism using the Rabbinic form of interpretation of scripture known as *remez* or hinting. Jesus was saying to the Sadducees that God was going to remove them from their place of authority. The stage was set for a bloody and violent showdown!

Today it is very hard to get a feel for the majestic building that was the Temple, when we only have the Wailing Wall as a witness. However, archaeological and historical data can be used to create a stunning picture of what today would undoubtedly be one of the wonders of the world. The Hebrew Bible reports that the first Temple was built in 957 BC by King Solomon, who reigned from c.970 to c.930 BC). As the sole place of Jewish sacrifice, the Temple replaced the portable tent sanctuary constructed in the Sinai Desert under the auspices of Moses, as well as local sanctuaries and altars in the hills. It was attacked and desecrated time and time again over the following centuries until finally around 20 BC, the building was renovated by Herod the Great, and became known as Herod's Temple. A full study of the Temple is impossible for the scope of a book like this so we will focus on Herod's Temple as this was the Temple frequented by Jesus and his disciples on many occasions.

The Jewish historian Josephus describes the colonnades:

> All the cloisters were double, and the pillars to them belonging were twenty-five cubits in height, and supported the cloisters. These pillars were of one entire stone each of them, and that stone was white marble; and the roofs were adorned with cedar, curiously graven. The natural magnificence, and excellent polish, and the harmony of the joints in these cloisters, afforded a prospect that was very remarkable; nor was it on the outside adorned with any work of the painter or engraver. The cloisters (of the outmost court) were in breadth thirty cubits, while the entire compass of it was by measure six furlongs, including the tower of Antonia; those entire courts that were exposed to the air were laid with stones of all sorts.
>
> *Jewish War 5. 5. 2*

The eastern portico was named after King Solomon and the part to the south, which overlooked the Valley of Kidron, was called 'Royal'. On the east side was the high corner which was quite possibly the pinnacle of the Temple mentioned in the story of the temptation of Jesus (Matthew 4:5).

There were a number of gates leading into the Temple. The outer four were the two Huldah gates or 'mole' gates from the south, which passed underneath the Royal Porch, the Gate of Susa to the east, still visible as the Golden Gate which was walled up by the Byzantines, and the main gate in the western wall, named the Gate of Coponius after the first procurator; it was decorated with the golden eagle as a sign that the Temple had been placed under the protection of Rome. I can't help but feel a slight discomfort every time I see a nation's flag taking pride of place at the front of a church meeting place, and my mind drifts to those Roman emblems claiming authority over the so-called house of God.

Anyone was allowed to enter the outer area, which was called the Court of the Gentiles. The actual Temple was enclosed by a balustrade, and at the entrances to it were warning notices, one of which is now in a museum in Istanbul. It says that foreigners have freedom of access provided they do not go beyond the balustrade which went all around the central edifice, which no uncircumcised could cross without incurring the death penalty!

Fourteen steps led through the Beautiful Gate to the Court of the Women where the poor boxes were, into one of which the poor widow cast her two mites (Luke 21:1–4). Another fifteen steps led up to the famous Gate of Nicanor, to which Mary had brought the child Jesus at the time of his presentation; this led through the Court of the Men to that of the priests, which had in its centre the altar for the burnt offerings, and to the left a large basin called the Brazen Sea resting upon twelve bulls cast in bronze. Further steps led up to the actual Temple, a comparatively small building. A priceless curtain, embroidered with a map of the known world, concealed from view what lay beyond, and none except the priest on duty was allowed to go farther. This was the VIP section, the ultimate green room, the Holy Place. It contained the golden altar at which incense was offered and next to it the seven-branched candle known as the Menorah and the table with the twelve loaves of showbread, which were replaced by fresh ones every Sabbath. Beyond it, behind another large curtain, lay the Holy of Holies, which none except the high priest was allowed to enter, and he only on the Day of Atonement. A special ornate stone designated the place where once the Ark of the Covenant had stood.

It is said that in Herod's Temple such an extraordinary amount of gold was used that during the siege of Jerusalem it melted into the rocks, causing the Romans to fulfil one of Jesus' prophecies that not one stone would remain on another as they scavenged between every rock and crevice for the melted gold. Some scholars believe that King Herod, desperate to buy the favour of the Jewish people and to make a name for himself, invested the equivalent of what today would be approximately three billion dollars!

So who was this upstart claiming to be the new Temple? How dare he claim he could rebuild this magnificent structure? He would have to be stopped at any cost and by any means, even if it meant sucking up to the hated Roman rulers. The Romans would not perform executions simply over violations of Jewish law, and therefore the charge of blasphemy with which they eventually accused Jesus would not have mattered in the slightest to Pilate.

Caiaphas' accusation would have to be based in one of the popular, though by no means held by all, views that Jesus was guilty not only of blasphemy, but also of proclaiming himself as the 'Davidic Messiah', understood by many, including the Zealot movement, as heralding the return of King David. This would have been an act of sedition and could indeed prompt Roman execution. It is important to understand that many believed that there would be two Messiahs, one in the order of Joseph, who would suffer, then another in the order of David who would rule. We find these beliefs' fulfilment in Jesus who suffered and yet rules, seated at the right hand of the Father, but who will also return in a greater fulfilment with every enemy as his footstool. It was time for a new high priest, not of the order of Zadok, not bent on his own personal gain or the abuse of the people. Rather this would be a high priest after the order of Melchizedek and his reign would be without end!

In Luke 16 we find a truly brilliant and surreal story that Jesus told about the Sadducees: a rich man lives in luxury, while at his gate lies a beggar named Lazarus. However, when the beggar dies, the angels carry him to Abraham's side, while when the rich man dies he is tormented in Hades. He cries out to Abraham for Lazarus to come and help him, only to be told that there is a great chasm between Heaven and Hell that none can cross. This is a truly brilliant, complex parable on so many levels, and one which raises many questions. In particular it strikes me that the rich man, who never helped Lazarus or saw his need in this life, is now asking Lazarus to serve him. He also wants someone to warn his five (remember that number) brothers so they will repent (*tshuva*, meaning to turn around from their current actions to embrace something better). In a beautiful example of the depth of Jesus' wisdom and communicative genius, he hints at his own coming sacrifice and his role as one returned from the dead to warn mankind.

The scriptures end with an awesome promise of Jesus stating that he is making all things new! The Greek word for 'new' here, *kainos,* is the word to renew, refresh and restore something to its original glory. Jesus' kingdom movement is all about piecing the world back together again; mortality swallowed up by immortality, Sodom and Gomorrah becoming like the very garden of Eden. What we so often consider as something for there and then, Jesus cries out is here and now. To know Jesus is everlasting life.

With that in mind, and if indeed Jesus did not intend for this to be a brief commentary on the underworld, what exactly is he trying to say in this parable? And why do I claim that this peculiar story is about the Sadducees? Here are a few clues.

In the parable Jesus mentions that the rich man 'dressed in purple and fine linen and lived in luxury every day'. In the ancient world purple was made from the secretion from a tiny shellfish from the Mediterranean ocean; it was a very difficult colour to produce and as such was worth a lot of money. It was typically used exclusively for royalty and the priesthood.

Colours were considered to have symbolic value within Hebrew culture, much in the same way as numbers were considered to contain more than simply quantitive value. We see the number three appear throughout the scripture to signify a totality and completeness, death and resurrection.

Red signified the earth (in fact the Hebrew word *adam* is from the same root as the word 'red'), and blue symbolised the heavens. Purple is a compound of blue and red, heaven and earth. Priests have always been viewed as the channel between heaven and earth and as such the priests were the main wearers of purple in Jesus' world. In Exodus 25–28, you will see that purple featured highly in the priests' clothing and all the interior decorations of the tabernacle. Jesus' first claim was that this man was of the elite, the top notch of society, and yet there's no mention of royalty or palaces. Jesus' audience would have quickly put two and two together.

The Rabbi goes on to say 'At his gate was laid a beggar'. Even today it is common, especially in developing or Catholic nations, for those in need to choose the gates of a church building to ask for alms. Why? Because there is a deep hope that those connected in some way to God will be the ones who hearts beat in time with he who gave his son. If there is mercy and compassion to be found, one would hope that it is here. We know that this was equally true in Jesus' day; we read stories of Jesus making a mud pie, which he then proceeded to smear on a blind man's eyes outside the Temple. Peter and John shock a crippled man – he is hoping for enough shekels to buy a pitta bread and falafel, and instead leaves 'walking, leaping and praising God'. This, however, isn't really enough evidence until we study the words Jesus uses. When he says 'gate' the actual word is '*pylon*'. This word was not used for ordinary gates, but for city and palace gates, and, most commonly for Jesus' audience, for the great Temple gates.

Still not convinced? When the rich man asks Abraham

to send Lazarus to warn his brothers he makes a point of mentioning five brothers. Remember I said that numbers are symbolic in Jewish thinking? Five is the number that symbolises grace. The grace of God wasn't something he suddenly invented with the death and resurrection of Jesus. Yahweh has always been the God of grace. If you read the chapters referring to the tabernacle the number five is all over the measurements and the descriptions of the divisions of the priests and even their clothing. The Torah is essentially five books, telling the people what this God is like and how to connect with him. In Jewish thinking Torah is grace, the law is grace; God chose the Jewish people not because of anything they had done to especially set them apart, but purely because of his love and mercy, and in turn they were called to display that love to the world and to be a light to the nations. We have already seen that the Sadducees only saw these first five books as authoritative and were even nicknamed as the 'people of five'. Is Jesus making a beautiful nuanced hint here to his audience? I think so. He blasts the so-called religious elite and the supposedly spiritual wealthy, claiming that they feast while there are others outside starving, longing for the crumbs that fall from their table.

Lazarus is the Greek form of the Hebrew name Eliezar, which means 'he who God hears'. Maybe the rich man in Jesus' parable could not hear or see the suffering on his doorstep, but God was certainly not blind. There is a subtle nuance in the parable in that the rich man isn't even named, whereas the poor man, he who in the eyes of the world was a nobody, is named many times.

Those who have a spiritual banquet seem blind

to Lazarus' suffering and Jesus uses the graphic and unpleasant image of wild dogs licking his sores. Dogs were a symbol to the Jews of the Gentile nations of that which was unclean, without a covenant. The Syro-Phoenician women, when she asks Jesus to come and heal her daughter, hears Jesus refer to them as 'little dogs'. This is shocking to our ears, but is actually simply the norm within that culture. However, Jesus is speaking about something else here. He is talking about the way that we look for something, anything to ease the pain, to soothe the stinging reality of life, sitting at the gate, hoping that there's something more, that maybe those who claim to have a connection with God will share some of that banquet with us. However when that relief doesn't seem forthcoming, where else can we find some help, some relief?

So often we see the hurting, destitute and hopeless letting the dogs lick their sores. Why is the drug addict shooting up? Why is the wealthy man trying to anaesthetise his pain with yet another possession that tomorrow will have lost its shine? Why is the businessman hiring yet another prostitute and waking up even lonelier than before? We have huge gaping sores, we look in all the wrong places, but ironically, often those who claim to have hope and the answers don't share what they have, or when they do, it is in such a way that it looks like crumbs falling from the table and so those with that aching gnawing pain in their gut, that hunger for what is real, leave completely unsatisfied.

A gate is built to keep people in, safe and sound in their own comfortable world and to keep others out. Every time we focus on our comfort and hold on with violent fanaticism to our interpretations, we build huge gates. In the end we get exactly what we want. The man wanted separation and that's exactly what he got. When he pleads with Abraham to send Lazarus to serve him in Hades, Abraham replies with a shattering statement: 'between us and you a great chasm has been set in place' .The chasm was in the rich man's heart. It was the gate that he fashioned in life and now he was simply living in the logical conclusion of such an attitude. He didn't need to die to be in hell, he was already forming hell on earth.

We desperately need to do some holy vandalism on the gates of religion that perpetuate the need for dogs to lick the sores of the world. We are the Sadducees so often – living in a world of spiritual wealth and privilege, we become deaf to the cries on our doorstep and numb to our responsibility to live as that channel between heaven and earth.

Jesus claims that he is the new Temple, the new dwelling place of God and that in him; we too are Temples of the Holy Spirit. The prophet Ezekiel saw a river that flowed from the Temple and the further it went the wider and more expansive it became. Everywhere that river went it brought healing and life – it pumped vitality, pulsated with change and transformed everything. The days are numbered for the Sadducee spirit in the church – there is no room for masks in this kingdom, no hiding behind designer suits, and no marriage with the empire. We must not be wooed by the wonder of comfort or the power of prosperity at any cost. We must remember that any authority we have is given to us by God above and we are simply stewards of his goodness. As followers of the Rabbi, it is imperative that we invite the world to this banquet and pour the biggest glasses of the wine of the spirit, showing them they don't need dogs to soothe the pain.

Let's stop holding on to our false notions of power and posturing. May we never be caught crying 'Crucify!' at what is true, good and of God because of our fear of losing what has been. It is time to remove the robes, allow ourselves to be covered in dust and embrace the real.

CHAPTER 5

THUNDER IN THE WILDERNESS: THE ESSENES

Billybob Joe from Texas and Lloyd Griffiths Jones from Kensington in London had an interesting relationship – both were ministers and though great friends, had a long running argument. It was over the accent of Jesus Christ. Billybob was emphatic that Jesus spoke English with a Texas twang, while Lloyd was horrified that anyone could imagine Jesus not speaking the Queen's English, 'My dear boy, I'm frightfully sorry but you are simply in error.' 'Aw you're all hat an' no cattle, you wait'n see when we is up yonder and you hear Jesus speak, brother you are gonna be throwin' a hissy fit, but be no better'n a no-legged man in a butt-kicking contest.' So it went on. Chance would have it that they died on the same day! There in heaven they ran up to Jesus, 'Lord, Lord, please tell us – we've been arguing our whole lives, tell us which one of us is right.' Jesus smiled at them and replied 'Buenos dias, mis amigos'.

Of course I jest, but I think we are in for many surprises on that day we find ourselves standing before the King. Is life not too short to pass by arguing over our minor differences, when we are quite probably wrong anyway?

Often in my travels I find myself connecting with Christian communities with a strong sense that they are called to retreat from 'the world'. Sometimes they live in stunningly beautiful farmland or surroundings with expansive acres, standing as bright and glorious testimonies to the wonder and beauty of this world, that to all intents and purposes they claim not to want to be a part of. Their children are all home-schooled, no TV is allowed and music that isn't 'Christian' is considered off-limits. The claim is usually that they are seeking a simpler, holier lifestyle. However, I can often see that this so called 'simple life' is anything but simple. It seems extremely rigid, and almost without fail we see the children desiring to rebel from it and to find out exactly what the off-limits world has to offer.

Are we supposed to be separate in this sense from the 'world'? Is this the message of the gospel? Are things really that black and white? Is it that God is a god of eternal love, rich in grace, mercy and loving kindness offering salvation and an eternity with him, unless somehow you don't say the exact words in the entrance prayer, or there's some doctrinal difference, in which case you will spend forever in torment? There are a million interpretations of what salvation really is, how to live the 'Christian life', rituals and rhythm guitars, choirs and chants, law and grace and here we are all over the place, trying to put the jigsaw puzzle together. It's so dangerous if we begin to think we have the monopoly on grace, the last will and testament to truth and that everyone else is wrong.

You may have been as disturbed as I was when in early 2011, American radio host Harold Camping stated that the Rapture and Judgement Day would take place on 21 May 2011, and that the end of the world would take place five months later on 21 October. For readers who may not be aware of what I mean by 'The Rapture' (sorry, I know it sounds like a horror movie or Stephen King novel), in broad-brushstroke terms it is the belief that God will take up into heaven his VIPs, his elect people, so that he can let loose his rage and wrath on mankind.

It is a fairly new theology within the history of Christianity, popularised through the Scofield Reference Bible, edited and annotated by the American Bible student Cyrus I. Scofield at the beginning of the twentieth century. It is widely accepted within American evangelicalism and to hold to any of the other interpretations held by millions of Christians around the world can almost be viewed as heresy by many of its adherents.

Camping, the president of the Family Radio Christian network, made the claim that 21 May would be the date of the Rapture and the Day of Judgement 'beyond the shadow of a doubt', suggesting that it would occur at 6 p.m. local time, with the Rapture sweeping the globe time zone by time zone. While some of his supporters claimed that around 200 million people (approximately 3 per cent of the world's population) would be 'raptured', it would be troubled waters from then on for the other poor 97 per cent! Camping had previously claimed that the Rapture would occur in September 1994. It is unclear if on this occasion he had also thought it to be 'beyond the shadow of a doubt'.

The vast majority of Christian groups thought Camping's predictions were ludicrous and we stood back in stunned disbelief as we saw billboards declaring the end of the world and people selling all their worldly possessions to fuel Camping's campaign. I remember being shocked at the traffic on social networks like Twitter and Facebook. Some big names in the evangelical world explicitly rejected Camping, and an interview with a group of church leaders noted that all of them had scheduled church services as usual for Sunday 22 May.

Following the failure of the prediction, media attention shifted to the response from Camping and his followers. On 23 May, Camping, rather than humbly saying, 'OK, so I got it wrong', stated that 21 May had been a 'spiritual' day of judgment, and that the physical Rapture would now be occurring on 21 October, simultaneously with the destruction of the universe by God. So, good news then! A few more months to choose whether to, as one of Canning's followers so graciously said on TV, 'turn or burn!' However, on 16 October Camping admitted to an interviewer that he did not know when the end would come, and 21 October passed without the predicted apocalypse.

We are fascinated by the idea that time is running out, that somehow we live caught in the thin line between the ages of what was and what will be. Ecclesiastes 3:11 states that God has put 'eternity in our hearts' – there is a realisation of something more, which is why the lines of John Lennon's 'Imagine' sound revolutionary in the first place. It's because, despite his melodic 'it's easy if you try', the truth is it isn't easy. In Jewish thinking heaven was not a 'then', but rather a 'now'. The desire was the Kingdom of God, heaven on earth, the age to come and all the groups had their views on this age to come, but none so much so as the Essenes.

 The people collectively referred to by various scholars as the Essenes comprised many separate but related religious groups of that era, sharing similar mystic, eschatological, messianic and ascetic beliefs. Although it is impossible to be sure, it is believed that the name comes from a Hebrew term *osey hatorah*, 'observers of Torah', or simply 'observers' because the exact etymology doesn't really give us any clues in Greek. This is another small but valid jigsaw piece in the likelihood that the Hebrew language was alive and well during Jesus' day and used in pious Jewish circles.

The Essenes were a nomadic people who flourished from the second century BC to the first century AD. It is highly probable that the vast majority of them came out of the now increasingly corrupt Zadokite priesthood, which would soon spawn the Sadducee movement. They were certainly much fewer in number than the Pharisees and the Sadducees – however, they were no less influential on the second Temple landscape, and hugely influenced thought and practices in the area where Jesus grew up.

Josephus records that Essenes existed in large numbers, and thousands lived throughout Judea. In his writings he claims to have had firsthand knowledge of them and speaks of them with great respect. He mentions their belief in the absence of personal property and of money and the belief in communality and commitment to a strict observance of the Sabbath. He further adds that the Essenes had a daily ritual baptism in water every morning, ate together after prayer, devoted themselves to charity and benevolence, forbade the expression of anger, studied the books of the elders, preserved secrets, and were very mindful of the names of the angels kept in their sacred writings. We have been able to learn a great deal of the possible life style of the Essenes, not only from the extensive writings of the historians Josephus and Pliny, but also since the landmark discoveries of the Dead Sea Scrolls, believed to have been written and preserved by the Essenes (or at the very least Essene-like) community at Qumran.

The accounts by Josephus and Pliny show that the Essenes led a strictly communal life – often compared by scholars to later Christian monastic living. Many of the Essene groups appear to have been celibate, but Josephus speaks also of another 'order of Essenes' that observed the practice of being engaged for three years and then getting married. According to Josephus, they had customs and observances such as collective ownership, electing a leader to attend to the interests of the group and obedience to the orders from their leader. Also, they were forbidden from swearing oaths and from sacrificing animals. They controlled their tempers and served as channels of peace, carrying weapons

83

only for protection against robbers. The Essenes chose not to possess slaves, but served each other and, as a result of communal ownership and living, did not engage in lawsuits. Both Josephus and Philo provide lengthy accounts of their communal meetings, meals and religious celebrations.

After three years' probation, newly joining members would take an oath that included the commitment to practise piety towards 'the Deity' and righteousness towards humanity, to maintain a pure lifestyle, to abstain from criminal and immoral activities, to transmit their rules uncorrupted and to preserve the books of the Essenes and the names of the angels. Their theology included belief in the immortality of the soul and that they would receive their souls back after death. Part of their activities included purification by water rituals, which was supported by rainwater catchment and storage. Ritual purification was a common practice among peoples of the Israeli landscape in this period and was thus not specific to the Essenes. Ritual baths are found near many synagogues of the period.

If it is correct to identify the community at Qumran with the Essenes (and that the community at Qumran are the authors of the Dead Sea Scrolls), then according to the Dead Sea Scrolls the Essenes' community school was called *Yahad* (meaning 'community') in order to differentiate themselves from the rest of the Jews, who were repeatedly labelled 'The Breakers of the Covenant'.

84

This motif of those who are in, and those who are out, of God's good graces can be found throughout their theology.

Many references to John the Baptist fit him into the Essene-like category of second Temple Judaism: at the very least we have to recognise that John was greatly influenced by this group and their teachings. They repeatedly referred to themselves as the 'children of light' getting ready to battle with the 'children of darkness', and their *modus operandi* was definitely one of retreat, isolation and self preservation. These communities or *Yahads* were places of great study and self-sufficiency. Their call was one of a *tshuva* (return and repentance) to the purity of the original Jewish community that left Egypt all those years before, living in the desert, following the cloud.

The Wilderness

To the Jew, the wilderness was the place to meet God. Everything about the wilderness reminded them of their honeymoon period with Yahweh. The word itself, *midbar*, literally means 'the place of speaking'. The root is *dbr* and gives birth to the words *dbir* ('flock') and *dbar* ('sanctuary'). The wilderness is where God gathers his flock into his sanctuary so that he can talk to them. The Essenes are, in a radical manner, saying, 'come back to that place where God can speak to us, challenge us, and gather us close to himself again.'

The Essenes practised full immersion baptism as a means of initiation into their movement. Full immersion baptism within even modern-day Judaism is reserved for proselytes converting to Judaism. For the Jew born into the promises and covenant of God, there were ceremonial washings. The archeology of the Temple Mount has revealed much evidence of *mikveh* baths to carry out these washings before entering the Temple courts. However, full immersion implied death to your old life and rebirth – something that was reserved for the Gentile coming into the Jewish faith. So could it be that this community and John the Baptist were saying, 'we've strayed so far away from the truth of who we are called to be that it is as if we were part of the heathen nations – we must repent, we must die, to be born again, because the kingdom of God is at hand!' Their message was sure to have powerful repercussions for the Jewish landscape of Jesus' day.

Many scholars believe that the disciples James and John were part of an extensive family that were greatly affected by the Essene movement. There are some interesting scriptures that refer to the disciple John's family being known personally by the High Priest, who as we have already noted, was at that time Caiaphas, the son-in-law of Annas. They were part of the priesthood and whether they actually were Levites or not, that was certainly the image they wanted to give. The Essenes would have been very well known to the priesthood, and as mentioned previously, a large percentage would have been disillusioned priests.

In Jerusalem around the Temple complex was the Essenes' quarter. Josephus refers to the 'Gate of the Essenes,' which appears to have been in the neighbourhood of Mount Zion. From the known landmarks in this description, we can conclude that this gate must have been on Mount Zion at the southern end of the western section of the First Wall,

86

just before it turned east across the valley toward Siloam. About 50 Essene priests may have lived in the southwestern quarter of Jerusalem between 30 BC and AD 70 . The Gate of the Essenes gave the community access to their ritual baths and latrines, which stood outside the city wall.

It is also interesting to note that when Jesus tells his disciples to go into the city and search out a man carrying 'a pitcher of water' to ask him permission to use his room to prepare for the Passover, it is very probable that Jesus is making reference to an Essene, as the Essenes were the only men likely to be carrying pitchers in this patriarchal culture. The Essenes believed in equality of the sexes and it was common for Essene men to be seen doing the tasks that generally only Jewish women would be expected to do. They were known for believing that in God's true community there was no distinction between rich and poor, slave and free, male and female but rather that they had all things in common; all things were to be shared and enjoyed together.

As we can see there were many similarities between the Essenes and the early church, including the communal meal, or love feast, sometimes referred to as the feast of the Messiah, that the Essenes shared daily where they would break bread together and drink wine together.

When the Messiah arrived, the Essenes wanted him to find people who were prepared to reestablish the true priesthood and true kingship of David and to battle the forces of spiritual darkness. Their mission was to prepare the way for the Messiah and to bring spiritual light to the world. The members of this highly organised society saw themselves as God's soldiers. They strengthened their bodies, minds, and spirits for the battle that would usher in the new age.

Is it time we realised that we are not accomplishing much by retreating to our cloisters and ghettos? Jesus is looking for leaven that affects the dough of mankind, mustard seeds that infiltrate every level of society, crashing through the concrete-like barriers of hate. As followers of the Rabbi, let's call people back to the true *dbar*, the true wilderness, the place of hearing God's voice, his sanctuary – but let's not stay there, selfishly hoarding his goodness to ourselves. No. Rather let's take the hands of everyone around us and show them into the promised land. Heaven on earth, the kingdom come!

CHAPTER 6

FIRESTARTERS: THE ZEALOTS

On 11 September 2001, nineteen terrorists from the Islamist militant group Al-Qaeda hijacked four passenger planes. On that fateful Tuesday morning the hijackers intentionally crashed two of these into the Twin Towers of the World Trade Center in New York City; both towers collapsed within two hours. Other hijackers crashed another American Airlines jet into the Pentagon in Arlington, Virginia. The fourth jet crashed into a field in Pennsylvania after passengers attempted to take control before it could reach the hijackers' intended target in Washington, D.C. Nearly three thousand people died in the attacks.

Although blame was laid at the feet of Al-Qaeda it took a further three years for the terrorist organisation to admit, with the then head of the group, the notorious Osama Bin Laden, citing the US's support of Israel, US troops in Saudi Arabia and sanctions levelled against Iraq as the motives for the attacks.

In 2001 I got engaged to my beautiful wife and most wonderful friend, Carolina. I was working with the international charity Youth With a Mission in a slum in Bogotá, the capital city of Colombia. Even in this small community the tribal lines were firmly drawn and people killed for what they believed in without thinking twice. Carolina and I worked with the ministry there, trying to intercept the children before they could grow up into street soldiers and vigilantes.

The slum was commonly known as *El cartucho* (a word referring to a gun cartridge) because of the violence and pain that was a daily reality for the inhabitants of this hell on earth. The first time I entered the vicinity in the back of a white beaten-up minibus, the hairs on the back of my neck stood up on end as the very atmosphere seemed to be permeated with darkness. All my senses were being simultaneously assaulted by the stench of rotten, burning rubbish on the pavement, the scenes of piles of bodies lying on street corners, and the sounds of fighting and angry voices mixed with a cacophony of music blaring from every direction.

Most days we were confronted with stories too horrific to repeat, of children forced to do unspeakable things and lives tragically ended before their time. Mafia, paramilitary, corrupt police and left wing groups held the area in constant upheaval and tension. It was the closest thing to hell on earth that I had ever experienced.

We went into this place of darkness on a daily basis and found much beauty in the ashes and flowers growing through the dirt. Jesus talked about the fact that when we give a cup of water in his name it is as if we give it to him and time and time again as I found myself looking into the eyes of a drug addict or child prostitute, a mother desperate to change for her child, I would see Jesus, looking back at me through their eyes.

It was a morning like any of the others when I stepped into Margarita's house to pick her up and take her to the ministry's nursery. Margarita was a beautiful nine-year-old girl with deep honey-coloured eyes and curly hair. She had a playfulness and life about her that contradicted the immense pain that she had already suffered in her short and troubled life.

It was imperative that we never entered the buildings alone but that we always had at least one other companion with us, but that day I broke with the protocol and stepped through the outer door by myself. The slum had once been the colonial Spanish sector of the city and, though now deeply marked by years of neglect, you could still see the colonial fingerprint in the balconies and shutters. Typical of the architecture of the time, the houses had a door that led to a small courtyard surrounded by rooms. Margarita shared a room with her whole family on the other side of the courtyard but on that particular day when I walked through the outer door, I was confronted by a small man with a thick black, knotted beard and hair hanging down over his face in matted unkempt dreadlocks and tangles. His eyes were full of darkness and burned with a hatred towards me that I had never experienced in my protected upbringing on the south coast of England.

He looked up at me and snarled out the words: 'What are you doing here? Don't you know, we kill people like you?' I noticed he had a large knife tucked into a belt keeping up the dirty, ripped jeans that must have been a number of sizes too big.

I'd like to pretend that I felt no fear and knew that heaven's army was surrounding me, but I'd be lying – never in my life had I felt adrenaline pumping through my body and fear creeping up my spine as at that moment.

'I'm ... I'm English ... Not American.' I managed to mutter.

'No soy gringo!'

Usually that bought some favour. They tended to be much more kindly disposed to the Brits, firstly because we didn't have the history of involvement in the fight against the drug trade, secondly because many knew of the British involvement in the fight for independence led by Simon Bolivar in the 1800s, but perhaps most significantly, because they love football! I hoped he would smile and say something along the lines of: 'Oh si! David Beckham!' We'd laugh, exchange a quick hug and I'd be on my way. But alas t'was not to be.

He snarled again ' I don't care, I kill people like you.' I looked behind me quickly trying to review my options. The doorway was now blocked by two other men who looked equally sinister and the enormity of the situation really hit me. I was in serious trouble. I looked down towards the hard stone floor and under my breath, with cold sweat running down my back managed to utter the words, 'Jesus ... please, please help me.'

Following my less than eloquent emergency prayer, everything became a bit of a blur. Without any recollection of how, or when, I suddenly found myself outside the complex, near to the minibus, which had been parked two short blocks away down the street. The minibus was surrounded by people and there seemed to be a lot of confusion. A young boy had been hit by a vehicle and as I would find out later, it seemed as if he'd broken his arm. As I walked towards the bus, my pace more like a run, I looked behind me, still dazed and confused, to see my three new friends stumble out of the building in shock and disbelief. They looked up at me, then towards the small crowd, turned and ran away down the street.

To this day I still cannot explain these events. It was as if God somehow picked me up, out of the enemy's hands and physically moved me into a place of safety. Please believe me – if I was making this up, I would be much more of a hero and less of a wimp and I would certainly try to make it easier to swallow, but that is what happened, so that is how I tell it.

In the same year, 2001 I travelled to the UK to visit friends and family during the later part of August and early September. It was, however, now time to go home. As always, in the search for flights I looked for the best deals and weeded the options down to either a flight back from the UK with Iberia, via Madrid, or a flight with Continental via Newark. Something inside me said to go for the Iberia flight via Madrid. The day arrived and I said a goodbye to family at Heathrow airport and off I set. The day was 11 September 2001.

The flight was like most – I whiled away the hours watching movies, eating, trying to sleep, watching movies, trying to sleep again, to no avail and finally arrived in Bogotá airport, exhausted, but full of joy because I was about to see my beloved fiancée. Stepping through the gate I saw her sparkling eyes and huge smile. She gave me a big hug, but then her expression changed as she looked at me and said, 'You have heard the news, right? We were all worried about you.' I hadn't heard the news. They don't tend to tell you about planes being hijacked while you are soaring a mile high in the very type of transport that has just been used to carry out the largest terrorist attack in human history. We arrived at the house where I was staying and put CNN on to see horrific images of destruction. It all seemed very surreal, like something from a big budget Hollywood movie, but it was real and we knew the world would never be the same again. Zealots have always existed and in Jesus' day, in very close proximity to where he grew up, Jesus would have been exposed to these self-styled 'soldiers of truth' that dotted the Jewish landscape.

 The Zealots or Kenai were in essence a religious/ political movement in first-century, second-Temple Judaism. They bitterly opposed Roman rule and taxation. Everything in these passionate partisans desired political freedom at any cost, and they sought to incite the people of the 'true Israel' to rise up, take up arms and rebel against the Roman empire and expel it from the Holy Land by force. There were numerous uprising and fights, from small-scale brawls to full-blown pushes for revolution, most notably during the Great Jewish Revolt (AD 66–70). These were guerrilla warriors, like those used by Che Guevara to overthrow the Cuban government in the 1960s. The Zealots have been described as one of the first examples of the use of terrorism, and one doesn't have to use too much imagination to picture them hiding out in caves like modern terrorists in Afghanistan.

Zealots were extremist Pharisees in one sense, and there is evidence to suggest that the Apostle Paul was born into a Zealot family, taking the Greek word *zelotes* that Paul uses for himself in Acts 22:3: 'I am a Jew, born in Tarsus of Cilicia, but brought up in this city. I studied under Gamaliel and was thoroughly trained in the law of our ancestors. I was just as zealous for God as any of you are today,' and Galatians 1:14: 'I was advancing in Judaism beyond many of my own age among my people and was extremely zealous for the traditions of my fathers.'

The church father Jerome claimed that Paul's parents were captured Zealots, forced by the Romans to pay their debt by working as slaves in a Roman family. According to Roman law, once the sentence was over the freed slaves automatically received Roman citizenship and this is the most widely accepted explanation as to why Paul, originally Saul, grew up as a Roman citizen.

There was no widespread resistance movement until shortly after Jesus' birth, when Judas of Gamla founded a radical Zealot movement in AD 6. The city of Gamla, built along a steep mountainside in close proximity to Jesus' home town, became a centre for the Zealot movement. However, these radicals certainly didn't see themselves as a new movement but rather traced their roots all the way back to the sons of Aaron, who they believed acted with great zeal when the children of Israel disobeyed God and fell into idolatry with such ease in the Sinai wilderness.

For generations, the Zealots violently resisted the emperor's authority. They longed for a Messiah who would lead a great holy army, destroy their Roman overlords, and reestablish Jewish rule in Israel. They taught that all foreign rule over the Jews was unscriptural. Serving Rome, whether by choice or as a slave, violated God's supreme authority, thus making any pacifists or collaborators accomplices in the crime and as accomplices, equally deserving of whatever punishment they decided to inflict.

It's no new revelation to us that for the most part the people were looking for a powerful politic Messiah who would drive out the Romans, just as Judas Maccabbeus had driven out the Greeks or King David the Philistines. They were looking for force, violence, pay back, revenge. Isn't that what we want deep down so often?

It was 10 August 2005, and we had gone to bed that summer's night in England unaware that in a few short hours our whole world would be shaken to the core. At 3:15 a.m. the telephone rang. Between sleeping and waking, I didn't quite make it to the phone in time. We had become accustomed to these late night calls – typically, Carolina's mum would call us to chat from Colombia completely oblivious to the fact that it was the middle of the night.

That night the phone rang again – this time I got it. It was Carolina's brother-in-law Ariel, usually very jovial, but his voice was downcast and serious as he told me that something terrible had happened to Carolina's younger brother. He went on to say that Diego had been shot in the street and they hadn't been able to stop the bleeding. He was gone.

We couldn't believe what we were hearing. Then the tears began to stream down our faces as sorrow broke through the shock. It all felt so surreal, so final and so wrong. Diego was everyone's friend. The girls loved his fun, live-life-to-the-full attitude and the guys wanted to be like him. How could this have happened?

He had not long finished his military service, fighting for and protecting his country in one of the toughest areas, facing daily the very real threat that it might be his last. When we had last visited he had told me that he wanted to become a pastor, and had many stories of how, on those dark, fearful nights in the Colombian jungle, he had been able to bring hope and security to his comrades through prayer and the stories from the Bible that had been his companion growing up.

He was no saint by the world's standards – he loved the ladies and very often drank more than he should. In his love for life he often found himself dicing with danger, but we never thought anything like this could happen. In time we would find out that a jealous friend had got into a brawl with him in a pool hall and Diego, never one to back down, had left him wishing he had never picked the fight. Later it transpired that this same 'friend' had paid a sixteen-year-old boy to shoot Diego in the street for the equivalent of eighty dollars. Carolina's older brother saw it all happen and ran after the youth, eventually together with the local police catching him and taking him into custody.

We hurriedly travelled to Colombia, with the extraordinary help of friends in the UK making it possible. We were numb, shocked, empty. It's very hard to put into words what you feel in these moments. I am not an angry, vengeful type of person, but I would be lying if I didn't say there were moments when I wanted the person who had done this to suffer, to really suffer. Not so much the youth who had been paid, who in many ways was another victim in this tragic story, but rather the guy who had in extreme cowardice sent him to carry out the deed.

There is a fine line in our desire for justice and our overflow of anger that longs for revenge. Suddenly turning the other cheek doesn't sound so great and an eye for eye seems like a fairer scripture.

At some point on that frightful night, Carolina's mum stood before her son's murderer.

With bitter tears burning her cheeks, she looked into his eyes and said, 'You've taken my baby from me. I have no idea why. My baby is gone and you took him from me.' Choking back the tears, and with the words almost fighting not to be pronounced in that cold dark cell, my mother-in-law cried: 'But I forgive you and if you let me I would accept you as my son.'

Shocking, scandalous forgiveness causes the endless cycle of revenge to cease and is the only way that we can begin to mend the world. Somehow we came to a place of peace too, even though we still desperately miss Diego and imagine all he would be doing today; we know he is safe and more alive than we are.

In Matthew 24, Jesus is prophesying exactly what will happen if his countrymen continue in the zealous pursuit of liberation through violence. He knows that it will end in desolation and pain, not the victory that they long for.

'Do you see all these things?' he asked. 'Truly I tell you, not one stone here will be left on another; every one will be thrown down.'

Matthew 24:2

And they were. Following the Jewish revolt, the Romans responded swiftly and mercilessly. Jerusalem was pillaged. Led by the future emperor Titus, the Romans surrounded the city, cutting off the food and water supplies of the inhabitants. They allowed the multitudes of Jewish worshippers to enter the city to celebrate the Passover feast, and then refused to allow them to go out. The Romans engaged in horrific brawls and street massacres with the Zealots, who were then ordered to retreat to the Temple to avoid heavy losses.

The Romans' eyes were on the Antonia Fortress which overlooked the Temple compound, providing a perfect point from which to attack the Temple itself. After several failed attempts to breach or scale the walls, the Romans launched a stealth attack, completely taking by surprise the sleeping Zealot guards, and took the fortress. The great, majestic Temple was eventually set on fire. Destroying the Temple does not seem to have been one of the goals for the Romans, as they would have loved to own such a magnificent piece of architecture – their desire was to seize it and transform it into a Temple of their own, dedicated to the Emperor and the gods. But the fire spread so quickly that very soon it was out of control. The Temple was destroyed, and because the huge amounts of gold used in its construction had melted into the cracks between the rocks, the Roman soldiers had to take the stones apart to salvage the gold, fulfilling Jesus' prophecy.

The Roman legions quickly crushed the remaining

Jewish resistance, and the few remaining Zealots managed to escape through hidden underground tunnels. The city was completely under Roman control by 7 September, and the Romans continued to hunt down all the Jews that had fled the city.

After the destruction of Jerusalem and the Second Temple in AD 70, 960 Zealots under the lead of Eleazar ben Yair took refuge by capturing the Roman fortress of Masada. A number of years ago I had the privilege of visiting Masada and seeing the impressive architecture, catching a sense of what it must have been like for that passionate remnant. Even today there is an eerie silence, looking out over the wilderness from that lonely, dusty plateau.

Rome sent the Tenth Legion to retake the stronghold, in what they thought would be a fairly easy and straightforward battle. Instead it took over three years and it is estimated that they had over 1,000 casualties in the process. The Zealots valiantly held the fortress even after the Romans invented new types of siege engines. Finally, in the third year of the siege the Romans were able to complete a massive siege ramp, which scaled one face of the mountain on which Masada sat. They then launched a full assault penetrating the walls previously impossible to touch. The Romans stormed in to capture the Zealots and prove their superior might, only to find that the fighters and their families were already dead. They had all, without exception, committed suicide. The Zealots, with all their fiery rhetoric, huge influence, guerrilla strategy and, well, zeal, did not have the means to change the world. The empire was not defeated and their Messiah had not come. Having rejected the spiritual kingdom and peace won at such a huge and bloody cost, that Jesus offered, they came to a tragic end.

Why is it that we think God somehow needs our help? When we cringe at the sight of our brothers and sisters picketing the next gay pride rally, or throwing stones at the abortion clinic, are they not, in their own minds at least, acting as 'soldiers for Christ', as 'zealots' for a cause'? At the core of this behaviour there is the erroneous belief that somehow the Almighty, Omnipotent Creator of the universe needs us to step in and help him.

Picture the scene, Jesus and his posse are in the Garden of Gethsemane. The Temple guard, police and soldiers arrive. It is a large enough contingency to warrant an officer to command them – they were, after all, terrified that a riot might begin.

> Jesus, knowing all that was going to happen to him, went out and asked them, 'Who is it you want?'
>
> 'Jesus of Nazareth,' they replied.
>
> 'I am he,' Jesus said. (And Judas the traitor was standing there with them.) When Jesus said, 'I am he,' they drew back and fell to the ground.
>
> John 18:4–6

This large regimented group of trained warriors stumbled over each other like drunkards. The Greek term for 'fell' here is *pipto*, which actually means to be violently thrust down, to fall prostrate, and to descend from a high place to the lowest. In an instant Jesus' simple words rendered them helpless. He was in complete control.

In steps Peter. Even after this display he's sure that Jesus needs his help. He draws a sword and strikes the High Priest's servant, cutting off his ear. Jesus rebukes him, and in Luke's version of the events, then proceeds

101

to heal the man's ear. Clearly Peter was a poor swordsman – he must have been aiming for the man's neck! I mean really, who tries to cut off an ear?

But we Christians still have a propensity to cut ears off! Not with actual swords and actual ears, of course. But the means can be just as violent and the damage just as permanent. Zeal to protect Jesus, his truths and his teachings, or more often than not, a certain interpretation of his teaching, cuts off the spiritual ears of the people around us. When we cut off people's ears with our words and actions, guess what? They won't hear us, they will only hurt. We desperately need the love of the Rabbi who comes and says today, 'No more of this!', who comes with love even for his accusers and attackers and brings healing.

General and later President of the United States Dwight Eisenhower said, 'I hate war as only a soldier who has lived it can, only as one who has seen its brutality, its futility, its stupidity.' Having served during World War II as the supreme commander of the Allied Forces in Europe, he had seen firsthand the desperate suffering it brought. He went on to say 'Every gun that is made, every warship launched, every rocket fired, signifies in the final sense a theft from those who hunger and are not fed, those who are cold and are not clothed.' Violence will only breed more violence, hate will only give birth to more pain. Just as Jesus warned them more than 2,000 years ago, his warning goes out to us today. Love your enemy. Because love never fails.

CHAPTER 7

WHITEWASHED: THE PHARISEES

To some who were confident of their own righteousness and looked down on everyone else, Jesus told this parable: 'Two men went up to the Temple to pray, one a Pharisee and the other a tax collector. The Pharisee stood by himself and prayed: "God, I thank you that I am not like other people – robbers, evildoers, adulterers – or even like this tax collector. I fast twice a week and give a tenth of all I get."

'But the tax collector stood at a distance. He would not even look up to heaven, but beat his breast and said, "God, have mercy on me, a sinner."

'I tell you that this man, rather than the other, went home justified before God. For all those who exalt themselves will be humbled, and those who humble themselves will be exalted.'

Luke 18:9–14

I f you are like me, and I'm just being honest here, you first read that story and thought to yourself, 'Thank God I'm not like that Pharisee.' If so, read on. The Pharisees are quite possibly the most misunderstood and misrepresented of all of the groups of Jesus' day. The Oxford English Dictionary defines a Pharisee as 'a self-righteous or hypocritical person'. But is this really fair, or do we need to review our thinking? Today we have extensive study resources available to us, including texts that no generation before us has had access to and we must allow this to help us properly review the biblical text and understand the world of Jesus. My fear, however, is that even with this new evidence in front of their eyes, some will still swear that black is white and vice versa.

The ancient Greeks told the tale of Procrastus, a kindly gentleman who would offer hospitality to any stranger passing through his village. He would invite them in and offer them the finest food and wine and the best room in the house. However, Procrastus had a sinister side – it transpired that in the guest room the visitor would find a bed that Procrastus would guide them toward and encourage them to rest their weary heads. This apparently model host would then proceed to ensure that the guest fitted exactly to the measurements of the bed – if they were too short they would have to be stretched; if they were too big, pieces of their body would have to be removed. Nothing was more important to Procrastus than the guest fitting exactly into the bed that he had prepared.

I believe we are all a little like Procrastus. We want to appear welcoming, postmodern, and willing to be challenged, and to a certain extent allow new ideas into our house, but when it really comes to the crunch we want to chop down those ideas to fit into our box and as a result we create mutant thoughts that cannot live too long. We need to let the Spirit open our eyes to the truth about the Pharisees as, though this may shock and scandalise you, Jesus was to all intents and purposes a Pharisee – or at the very least, this was the group with whom he held the closest affinity.

So let us start with the basics. As we have already seen, the Pharisees came out of the group of freedom fighters known as the Hasidim. We can trace both their movement and that of the Zealots back to a theological fork in the road following the liberation of Israel. As mentioned before, the majority of the people who returned from the Babylonian exile were traditionalists, conservatives, and somewhat right-wing in their thinking, with a strong affinity with Jerusalem and Judea, the area in which they settled. Many other Jews decided to stay in Babylon, preferring not to exchange one form of slavery for another. However, following the Maccabean revolt they were free to return to their homeland.

But where should they go? The land of Samaria was packed with Samaritans and they weren't welcome there. The Judeans saw them as outsiders. They had maintained the original, fiery faith of the prophets and their forefathers and were seen as wild charismatics. These Jews believed in prophecy, in healing, they raised their hands when they worshipped, and there are even stories of them shaking under the power of God. As far as the Judeans were concerned these were *nudniks*, fools, crazies. To the Judeans at the time of the exile God was through with dealing directly with his people. There was no more prophecy, there would be no more great miraculous displays of God´s power. They

105

had substituted the Temple for the presence, the rituals for reality.

Our friends returning from Babylon needed somewhere that they could practise and develop their faith and there would only be one suitable area – Galilee.

 The Sea of Galilee lies on the ancient Via Maris, which linked Egypt with the northern empires. The Greeks, Hasmoneans and Romans founded flourishing towns and settlements on the land-locked lake including Gadara, Hippos and Tiberias. Josephus was so impressed by the area that he wrote, 'One may call this place the ambition of Nature.' He also reported a thriving fishing industry at this time, with 230 boats regularly working in the lake.

The Sea of Galilee is the largest freshwater lake in Israel and the lowest freshwater lake on Earth. After the Dead Sea it is the lowest lake in the world! It is fed partly by underground springs, although its main source is the Jordan River, which flows through it from north to south.

Extensive archaeological discoveries indicate that Galilee was largely unpopulated at the return of the rest of the exiled community in approximately 166 BC. We do know, however that on the other side of the Sea of Galilee was the thriving Decapolis, the ten cities, which we shall look at shortly. But for now suffice it to say that the huge influx of Jews came into this area of Northern Israel toward the west of the great Gennesarat.

This would be the home and stronghold of the Pharisee movement, the Bible belt, and the three towns of Capernaum, Korazin, and Bethsaida are sometimes called the 'gospel' (or orthodox) triangle, because they form a triangle, with the points about three miles apart. The Bible indicates that most of Jesus' miracles were performed in the three towns of this area.

Certainly not all people who lived in this fertile area were religious or even Jewish. But it is clear that most inhabitants of the sea's northwestern side were very religious, a fact supported by archaeological finds of many synagogues discovered there. As previously mentioned, Galilee was not a backwoods region; the international trade route, the Via Maris or the Way of the Sea, ran through this area near Capernaum. Israel had always lived in a land that connected great empires. The whole world knew of them because the trade routes passed through their country, and as the nations of the world passed by, Israel could obey God's command and be his witnesses. Jesus also chose this crossroads area for ministry so that his message could be heard by people from around the world. And he chose Capernaum as his home to fulfil the prophecy that the Messiah would live in Galilee by 'the way to the sea' (Matthew 4:13–15). Located on the shore of the sea, this major town was home to fishermen, farmers, a Roman garrison, and a customs house (where tax collectors worked). Capernaum had a large synagogue, the remains of which are beneath the ruins of a later synagogue. Many of the New

Testament stories about Jesus took place here. Jesus' disciple Matthew, a tax collector, came from this town.

In Matthew 9 we read about the healing and forgiveness of a paralysed man, the calling of Matthew, the healing of the woman with the issue of bleeding, the raising of the dead girl, healing of the deaf and mute by casting out the demonic spirit controlling him. All these amazing things happened in Capernaum.

Korazin was a town located three miles north of Capernaum. Although this was one of the towns where most of Jesus' miracles took place, the Bible records no specific visit of Jesus to this town. It was large and prosperous and had a synagogue. Its economic pursuits included the processing of olives.

The last of the towns in the orthodox triangle is Bethsaida. We read in both John 1:44 and John 12:21 that Peter, Andrew and Philip were all successful young fishermen from Bethsaida. This town was located on the northern end of the sea near the mouth of the Jordan River, and is the historic site where Jesus fed the five thousand. In Mark 8:22 we read about one of the occasions on which he healed a blind man. The ruins of Bethsaida are now being uncovered for the first time, revealing a prosperous town constructed of basalt, a black rock common to the area. This was the home of the Pharisees – their 'hood.

The Pharisee movement was by no means monochrome, and to paint them all with the same brush would be similar to looking at all branches of evangelicalism as one uniform system and practice. There were huge variations within the movement, way beyond the scope of this book. However to give a broad-brush overview of the Pharisees we can look at the two ends of the spectrum and gain a better understanding of some of the thoughts and debates flying around during the time of Jesus.

The School of Hillel and the School of Shammai

The Pharisaic attitude is perhaps best exemplified by a story about Hillel the Elder, who lived at the end of the first century BC. A man once challenged the sage to explain the law while standing on one foot! Hillel replied, 'That which is hateful to you, do not do to your friend. That is the whole Torah; the rest is commentary – go and study it.' Jesus would appear to be making a reference to this in one of the most famous and revolutionary sermons ever given, the Sermon on the Mount' – however, Jesus flips it over to the positive: 'So in everything, do to others what you would have them do to you, for this sums up the Law and the Prophets' (Matthew 7:12). This would not be the first time that it would appear that Jesus sided with the school of Hillel.

Hillel was born, it is traditionally believed, in 110 BC. Renowned within Judaism as a sage and scholar, he was the founder of the 'House of Hillel' and of a dynasty of sages who stood at the head of the Jews living in the land of Israel until roughly the fifth century. He is popularly known as the author of two sayings:

'If I am not for myself, who will be for me? And when I am for myself, what am "I"?' and 'If not I, then who? If not now, then when?'

Shammai was a contemporary of Hillel and headed up the Sanhedrin for some time. It seems that Shammai Pharisees congregated in greater numbers within Judea and around Jerusalem. They stood in opposition to Hillel on many points. In the record of the Talmud there are over 316 issues that they debated over – basically every command of God! However, there are really only four main areas recorded by the two opponents as having particular importance.

These were:

1. **Admission to Torah study.** The House of Shammai believed only the most worthy of students should be permitted to study Torah. The House of Hillel believed that Torah could be studied by anyone.
2. **Lies.** One of the debates was over whether one should tell an ugly bride that she is beautiful. Shammai said it was wrong to lie, and Hillel said that all brides are beautiful on their wedding day.
3. **Divorce.** The House of Shammai held that a man may only divorce his wife for a serious transgression, but the House of Hillel allowed divorce for even trivial offences, such as burning a meal!
4. **Hanukkah.** The House of Shammai held that on the first night eight lights should be lit, and then they should decrease on each successive night, ending with one on the last night; while the House of Hillel held that one should start with one light and increase the number on each night, ending with eight.

Shammai's positions tended to be far stricter than those of the House of Hillel. The principles of the House of Shammai in relation to foreign policy were similar to the views of the Zealots, and as a result they found a great deal of support with that group. Many historians would see the Zealots as extreme Shammai Pharisees. As public hatred for the Romans grew over the first century, Shammai's teachings became more popular and his school of thought gradually gained the upper hand and controlled the Pharisaical vote within the Sanhedrin. Although following the destruction of the Temple Hillel's school would become dominant, and went on to be the founder of modern-day Rabbinic Judaism, at this time it took a back seat.

Like the Zealots, the Pharisees were an offshoot of the Hasidim movement. *Perushim* in Hebrew means the 'set apart ones'. The name was clearly chosen not only to denote that they were set apart both from the Sadducees and their Hellenistic tendencies and the Zealots' adherence to violent revolt, but also to reflect their belief that they had been set apart for God. According to Josephus they received the respect and admiration of the people, as opposed to the Sadducees. They were loved. Little Jewish boys grew up wanting to be Pharisees.

The major difference between the Pharisees and the Sadducees was that Pharisees believed that the laws and traditions of the Jewish people must be upheld in the face of assimilation with the Gentile overlords. They were considered the most accurate expositors of Jewish law. In general, while the Sadducees were conservative, wealthy, aristocratic monarchists, the Pharisees were from every type of background, popular and democratic.

Pharisaic views were non-creedal and non-dogmatic. I

expect that surprises you, as we have the tendency to see them as incredibly dogmatic, and granted some factions most probably were, but none of the key Rabbinic texts are devoted to singular theological issues as such; these texts are concerned primarily with interpretations of Jewish law, and anecdotes about the sages and their values. Unlike much of Christian theology, there isn't an obsession with the afterlife – eternal life was very much wrapped up in their understanding of the here and now. Only one chapter of the Mishnah even hints at eternal life as most Christians would understand it; it asserts that there are three kinds of people who will have no share in 'the world to come': those who deny the resurrection of the dead, those who deny the divine inspiration of the Torah, and Epicureans, who, interestingly, were those who denied divine supervision of human affairs. The Jews of Jesus' day and orthodox Jews today see God's hand in everything – all is spiritual and comes from God's generous heart, and all is to be enjoyed in the manner that he has described.

The idea of a separate market for 'Christian music' and so-called 'secular music' would have been absolutely foreign and ludicrous to Jesus and his audience. The Kingdom of God was about that mustard seed affecting the culture, affecting every sphere of influence, not producing, lesser, ghetto versions of what the world was already doing and doing better! Rather, the Kingdom movement was to lead the way.

When I began to understand more about Jesus' ministry I was shocked that it took place in such a small geographic area and over such a short period of time. He didn't try and make his way to the epicentres of culture, religion or commerce, and yet his short ministry has changed the face of the earth and his impact has been greater than any other who has ever lived! However, we would be wrong to think that Jesus lived out his ministry in a backwater with an insignificant landscape. In Capernaum excavated black rock shows the synagogue of Jesus' time, which archeologists have identified as the largest synagogue of the ancient world until approximately AD 400. This wasn't some hillbilly, off-the-beaten-track place. Here was the cream of the religious crop – this was the Oxford, the Cambridge, the Harvard of its time as far as Judaism was concerned. Jesus was not a peasant who went to only the poorest of the poor and the outcasts, although he did lift up the 'least of these'. However, he also went to touch the hearts and minds of the top of society, the intellects, movers and shakers and policy-makers. He knew that if he could transform and touch that area, he could create a ripple effect that could change the world, and history shows us he was right.

It was the Pharisees who were the evangelists of their day. They took literally the mandate to be witnesses to the world around them. They were the kind of people who would grab the message and run with it, people of passion and zeal who would confront persecutions, stoning and hardships for their beliefs. This shouldn't surprise careful readers of Acts. Luke notes earlier that many priests, Pharisees, and thousands who were 'zealous for the Law' were part of the first generation of Jesus-followers (Acts 6:7; 15:5; 21:20). Paul did not stop being a Pharisee when he began to follow Jesus! In fact on many occasions he makes reference to this and is proud of being a part of this group.

If at the beginning of this chapter you, like me, thought to yourself, 'Thank God I am not like that hypocritical, self-righteous Pharisee,' then this parable speaks directly to you

113

and me. It addresses those who were 'confident of their own righteousness'. Is this not exactly what we display when we judge the Pharisee that Jesus is showing as judgmental? Can we really claim to be any better, when essentially we are doing exactly the same thing?

Within the church of Jesus Christ it is very easy for us to point fingers and accuse each other of being modern-day Pharisees. We can all think we've got it right and everyone else has it wrong. We can all be Pharisees, in the modern understanding of the term, but quite frankly, we've got it wrong. When Jesus told this story, his audience would have been both shocked and deeply saddened to see this Pharisee, a highly respected man of God, acting in such a way.

There was a debate going on at the time of Jesus with regard to something known as *kavanah*. This was a term that referred to the intent of the heart. The school of Hillel insisted that any act of worship, following of Torah or sacrifice must be done out of a heartfelt love for Yahweh and a desire to obey and please him. Their stance was that it simply wasn't enough to be seen doing the right thing, or to tithe the exact amounts and attend synagogue and the various feasts. Your heart had to passionately be in pursuit of God and his ways, and desire with everything to follow his precepts. We see this type of *kavanah* displayed in Psalm 119, written by King David. This is the longest of all the psalms, and is dedicated to his passionate love of God's word, laws and ordinances. It simply was not enough to go through the motions, seemingly being obedient – you had to feel the fire.

The school of Shammai didn't agree. They believed that the simplest act of obedience, of choosing to do what Yahweh said even if you didn't want to, was acceptable. So you went to the Temple, you did your thing and even if you didn't really want to be doing it God looked down and you still got your points.

Of course both views have wisdom and truth all over them but human nature just loves to argue instead of seeing that both are right and we are all partly wrong. This was a serious issue in Jesus' day and it would seem that Jesus is speaking into the debate.

We already know that there was quite a lot of diversity within the Pharisee movement, but let's break it down even more. According to the Babylonian Talmud there were actually seven categories of Pharisee. The first was the superficial Pharisee or the *sheikmi*; which literally means 'shoulders'. This group was frequently called and known as hypocrites. The shoulder reference has interesting nuances – it can be taken to mean burdening people with things they themselves are not willing to carry. The criticism against this group of Pharisees, the hypocrites, was that they only did what they did for what they thought they were going to get out of it.

We can often see double standards in this kind of expression of faith. I have friends who have grown up in a protected Christian environment and only ever listened to so-called 'Christian' music. Quite frankly, they are often anaesthetised to the radical and subversive nature of Jesus and his insurgent movement. Other friends who have grown up in very dark and destructive atmospheres are shaken to the core at the attractive and powerful nature of Jesus.

Carolina and I happened to be visiting a Christian missions base in a Latin American country the day after the death of the Queen of Salsa music, Celia Cruz. The news report gave a summary of her life, praising her faithfulness to her husband and the joy her music had brought. They ended the report saying that they were sure that she would be preparing the parties in heaven now, something which instantly warmed my spirit. The thought of that larger-than-life lady spinning the angels around on God's great dance floor just seemed right. Not so to our companions, who through gritted teeth muttered, 'More like the parties in hell!'

First off, I'm pretty sure there aren't going to be parties in hell. And secondly, who did they think they were, saying where Celia Cruz would be? Why were they so sure? And why did they almost seem smugly pleased by it? I felt sick to my stomach. All I could reply was that I certainly hoped she'd be there adding *sabor latina* ('latin flavour') to the liturgy!

I could tell they were less than impressed that we knew the songs and lyrics to this 'worldly' music! Most of these missionaries looked very disdainfully on any artistic expression that didn't have some blatant Christian message emblazoned on it. A painter could not paint a beautiful landscape without having to whack a scripture on it – it didn't even seem to matter what it was! It could be a painting of a sunset over a peaceful seascape and in the corner the scripture, 'Vengeance is mine, sayeth the Lord', but as long as the scripture was there it was kosher. So-called 'Christian' music could be full of unbelief and sentimental nonsense, but if it mentioned God and Jesus it was OK, while often the so-called 'worldly' music was being used as a prophetic voice to speak out on the issues that were really on God's heart. Jesus said that if the crowds didn't speak for him, then the rocks would cry out. So often God has also used rock stars to cry out, in place of an, at times, shockingly quiet church.

The conversation quickly moved on to the movie that a group of them had seen the previous night. Their accolades for this movie were flowing as they praised the storyline, the actors and the drama. It turned out that it was a movie specifically about unfaithfulness, lies and adultery. The interesting thing was that no one seemed to think anything was wrong or out of place in feeding your mind with images, storylines and dramas focused around these subjects, while listening to music that might make your hips move a certain way but was about love, life and positivity was somehow going to destine you to burn.

Leo Tolstoy once said, 'Hypocrisy in anything whatever may deceive the cleverest and most penetrating man, but the least wide awake of children recognises it and is revolted by it, however ingeniously it may be disguised.' The masks of hypocrisy, the suits, the voices don't fool anyone but those who assume them, believing they will somehow make them appear more holy.

A second type of Pharisee was the bent-down Pharisee, the *nikphi*; which literally meant 'stumbling'. These were those criticised for simply not practising what they preached. They stood on the street corners and made a very big deal about their righteousness. The third was the extreme Pharisee or *qitzai*, which literally means 'bleeding'. The reason they got this nickname was because they were so afraid of being drawn into sin by something they saw, such as lusting after a beautiful lady passing by or coveting their neighbour's latest chariot, that they looked down and were constantly bumping into things!

The fourth type was the announcing Pharisee, the *dukai*, which means 'pounding'. The criticism against this group was not for their actions – they did what was good and right. Their problem was they really wanted you to know about it. You've seen the person who makes a big deal about writing out a large cheque to pop in the offering, the one who uses an elaborate voice and words that they would never ordinarily use when they preach or pray in public. Their heart may be in the right place and they really may have a desire to please God – they just really enjoy the kudos that goes with it.

The fifth type were the accounting Pharisees. Everything they did was in an attempt to earn points, to somehow try to be the best they could be, thinking that they could buy God's love. Therefore every day that they fasted, every shekel tithed, every early morning prayer session was seen as a step towards their acceptance in God's eyes. They were good men but lived in a constant state of insecurity.

The sixth type, which was also by far the vast majority, were the Pharisees of fear. These Pharisees lived with such a reverential awe of Yahweh and such a deep respect of Torah that everything within them was geared towards desperately trying to do what was right. They were in awe that God had chosen them to be the light to the world and they took it seriously. Fires burned in them – they were passionate. They believed in national salvation, if everyone would just turn back to Yahweh and follow his laws and precepts.

You've probably noticed a progression in the list. We started with the ultra-negative hypocrites and now we have worked our way up to the immensely respected Pharisees who feared the Lord and lived for him. However it doesn't

118

stop there. One other group still remains and they were known as the Pharisees of Love.

These Pharisees had come to such a depth of relationship with God that essentially his love and character had become their driving motive. Everything they did was done because they had been arrested by love. Generally these were the Rabbis. It is very difficult to describe the kind of love and respect that the people had for these Pharisees. It would be true to say that Jewish parents longed for their little boys growing up to become Rabbis of this calibre – men of God who loved Yahweh with all their mind, their hearts and strength and out of that love were able to love their neighbour as themselves. They were often called Pharisees of Pharisees, a term Paul used to describe himself.

In the Gospels we see the Pharisees warning Jesus of danger (Luke 13:31). Jesus refers to them as 'righteous persons' in Luke 15:7, and in Acts 5:34–39 Gamaliel, one of the greatest Jewish teachers of all time and a renowned Pharisee, stood up for the fledgling messianic movement. And we have already noted that a very large number of Pharisees came to faith in Jesus following the resurrection. However, we also see Jesus' harsh criticisms of the Pharisees.

We really must understand these criticisms as an 'in-house' debate between different factions, and never as Jesus hitting out against the movement as a whole. Every Rabbinic school and the different groups within the Pharisee sect were known to, at times, bitterly oppose each other, on occasions using very colourful language.

In Matthew 23 we see Jesus getting pretty heated with the first group of Pharisees that we studied, the hypocrites:

'Woe to you, teachers of the law and Pharisees, you hypocrites! You are like whitewashed tombs, which look beautiful on the outside, but on the inside are full of the bones of the dead and everything unclean. In the same way, on the outside you appear to people as righteous but on the inside you are full of hypocrisy and wickedness.'

When we hear the word 'hypocrite' we have all kinds of preconceived ideas about what that word means, but in Jesus' day it was essentially a part of the culture of the Greek theatre – the 'hypocrites' were a certain type of masked actor. They would even occasionally use techniques and devices to distort and change the sounds of their voices. So Jesus is actually saying of this group of Pharisees that they are actors – they don't show their true selves.

Jesus uses a term in his parable about the Pharisee and the tax collector referring to them 'going up to worship' – this is a Jewish way of talking about both ascending the 'hill of the Lord' metaphorically, as one went 'up' to meet with God, but also physically, as it was a journey of ascent up to the Jerusalem Temple. The Jewish term is *tefillah,* and it is used to describe one's necessity to judge oneself in relation to God, to see ourselves as we really are in the awesome light of his glory and goodness. It is the contemplative act of getting your heart in the right place to meet with the King of the Universe, repenting, asking for forgiveness and humbling yourself under the mighty hand of God. That is what these two players in Jesus' tale are doing.

The Temple courts would fill up twice a day at 9:00 a.m. and 3:00 p.m. for the morning and afternoon sacrifices. Following the blood of the sacrifice being thrown on the great altar, as wisps of smoke rose up mingling with the aroma of the anointing oil and as thousands of worshippers huddled together, crying out to God to remember his covenant, the place would become silent as the high priest walked into the sanctuary to represent the nation. It would appear that Jesus is referring to this incredibly sacred moment when he speaks of the Pharisee bringing out his verbal list of achievements, giving himself a very loud and public pat on the back, while the tax collector beats his chest and weeps before God in this moment of awe and recognition of the greatness of Yahweh.

Jesus further shocks his audience when he says 'This man went home justified before God.' Tax collectors were looked on as worldly, frivolous, immoral and selfish thieves, collaborating with the despised Roman occupiers, while the Pharisees were greatly loved and respected. If Jesus was telling the story today, perhaps a modern equivalent would be 'The Pope and the Pimp'!

There is something curious about sheep and goats in the Middle East. As far as appearances go they can be remarkably similar – however, in characteristics they are worlds apart. A sheep knows its shepherd's voice, and obeys and depends on the shepherd and sheepfold, its community. A goat does its own thing, looks for its own food, doesn't need the community and is willing to steal wherever it goes. So the shepherd would separate the sheep from the goats, and this forms the background to one of Jesus' most dramatic parables, in which he separates those who know him from those who don't (Matthew 25:31–46).

In the kingdom we can look the part. We can say 'Amen' in all the right places, but if we truly desire to walk in the dust of the Rabbi then the real question is, do we know him? Have we been arrested by his love? Can we live with that love bursting forth in our hearts like the Pharisees of love? Jesus is looking for those who really know him.

CHAPTER 8

THE WORLD OF THE RABBI

Jesus, or rather Yeshua Ben Yosef, was not a Christian. He was a Jewish man who grew up in a Jewish family and followed Jewish customs and rituals. He said the things that Jews said and ate the food that Jews ate. Jesus functioned as a Jewish Rabbi – yes, a Rabbi of incredible strength and determination, awesome depths of insight and outstanding discipline and practice. However, Jesus was a man!

The term 'Rabbi' or' Rabboni' means quite simply an honoured man. It is believed that at the time of Jesus this was something to be achieved by lifestyle, wisdom, experience and fruit of ministry, as opposed to our modern idea of ordination. In modern-day Judaism a Rabbi must be ordained or receive *shmicha* (meaning 'authority') – in Jesus' time it was not an office that relied on ordination, simply because that would have been an affront to the Temple priesthood, and no God-fearing Jew was going to challenge the institution of the Temple. However, you would find people who were unbelievably talented and learned in the Torah and the *haftorah* (basically meaning 'the rest' of scripture), which comprised the oral law and sayings of the sages passed down throughout the ages. These people were known as Torah teachers. The Torah teachers had a phenomenal ability to take the words of God and communicate great truths in simple ways. These were great theologians, remarkable communicators and lived, for the most part, godly lives, causing them to be highly respected.

Generally they would travel from place to place teaching in the villages, synagogues and the various schools of the disciples. They were however, rather limited in the scope of their teaching, the reason being that they were not permitted to take scripture and to form doctrine. You would not hear a Torah teacher claiming to have come up with a new interpretation or revelation from the scriptures. What you would hear them doing is expounding on what Rabbi so and so said or in the name of Rabbi so and so. They could not make their own interpretation based on their opinion or leading of the Spirit, even in community with other Torah teachers. The Rabbis called this *midrash* but Torah teachers could not form new *midrash*. That simply was not permitted.

Midrash was the domain of the Rabbi, and in Jesus' time there were very few Rabbis whom we get the chance to hear of. As mentioned previously, it was not considered an office as such. However, it was certainly something that people eagerly aspired to. In the world of the Pharisee it was the pinnacle of achievement, and to the multitudes that they influenced it was perhaps considered the most honourable vocation one could desire.

The classic method that a Rabbi would use to teach would be to say 'it is written...' or 'you have heard it said ...' and then go on to say 'but I say to you...', a pattern that Jesus uses frequently in the Sermon on the Mount. Here Jesus is bringing a new interpretation of the ten commandments, creating *midrash*, a revelation of what God really intended. He is not behaving as a Torah Teacher, but rather as a Rabbi with authority. The only other Rabbis we hear of who did this kind of thing at the time of Jesus were Hillel and Shammai, Hillel being the youngest in receiving this 'authority' at the age of sixty! That's why people were so shocked at Jesus' teaching, and why we read time and again of people asking where he got his authority from. It was unbelievable to the ears of Jesus' listeners that someone so young and apparently unlearned in the great schools could possibly have attained the wisdom and insight to be able to do what only the greatest of Rabbis had previously done.

This concept of authority was known as *shmicha*. For a Rabbi to receive *schmicha*, at least two other Rabbis would have to come and lay their hands on them and say something along the lines of 'This is my beloved son, in whom I am well pleased'. We read in all the Gospels about Jesus' baptism experience, in which God the Father speaks these words over him, and the Holy Spirit descends on him – what greater testimony and affirmation could there be than that of the voice of the Heavenly Father himself declaring Jesus as Rabbi?

I had the privilege of hearing a great Bible teacher named Ray Vander Laan talk about his time studying in Jerusalem. His Jewish teacher asked him, 'You Christians,' (although they don't use the term 'Christians' but rather *noztrim,* which means a shoot or offshoot) 'where does your Rabbi Yeshua receive his *shmicha,* his authority?' He responded that in all honesty he really did not know. The professor, being an honourable and godly man, responded, 'My son, you are too humble.' Then turning to the class, the professor said, 'My children, this Christian follows the only Rabbi in all of history who received his *shmicha* directly from *Hashem,* directly from Almighty God!' Ray went on to say how suddenly that revelation hit him like a lightning bolt, and he could hold his head up high in wonder and awe that our Rabbi Jesus the Messiah didn't simply get his credentials from other great men or women of history, but rather directly from the maker of the universe, the King of Glory, Almighty *Baruch Hashem,* Papa God. This same Jesus would go on to breathe on his disciples and send them out saying, 'All authority in heaven and on earth has been given to me. Therefore go and make disciples of all nations, baptising them in the name of the Father and of the Son and of the Holy Spirit' (Matthew 28:18–19). We follow the greatest Rabbi and walk in his authority, speaking in his name!

All Rabbis with *schmicha* prophesied and were known to heal the sick and to perform remarkable miracles. I don't know what that does to your preconceptions of the religious leaders of Jesus' day, or how it affects your theological paradigms, but extensive historical sources and oral stories show that all the Rabbis moved in the power of God and were used in signs and wonders. There is a plethora of stories that could be cited, and that mirror many of the miracles of Jesus. Hanina Ben Dosa was greatly used to heal the sick and there are stories of him turning vinegar into oil. Then we find stories about Rabbis who perhaps didn't calm storms but were able to cause them – Hanina Ben Dosa was known to cause rain, as was Rabbi Akiba. There are approximately 170 miracles recorded in the Mishnah, and though some may seem a little bizarre to us, for the most part they sound as if they could have come straight out of the pages of the New Testament, involving healing, casting out demons, control over the laws of nature and the like.

I used to believe that the stunning miracles that Jesus wrought, filling me with wide eyed awe, were done because he was the son of God. Similarly I believed that nothing was impossible for Jesus because, well … he was God, right? I used to think that people's astonishment was because Jesus was one of a kind and that they had never seen anything like that before. That simply wasn't the case. He was following in the tradition of the prophets and other men and women who had been used by God throughout the Old Testament and in the intertestamental period. He didn't do those things because he was the son of God – rather, he did them to show us what it meant to live controlled by and under the influence of the Holy Spirit, as a man fully human, yet fully divine.

There were, however, a number of miracles that were unique to Jesus and it would appear that the purpose of John's Gospel was to reveal these miracles (see John 20:30–31). These were those that proved and pointed out to all with eyes to see and ears to hear that he was indeed the Messiah, the son of the living God. We do not read about other Rabbis raising the dead after three days, as it was believed that the spirit of a person would depart to Sheol after three days and that following that departure it was impossible for someone to be raised.

127

Only the Messiah would have that kind of authority. It was also considered impossible to cleanse a leper of their leprosy, as they believed that leprosy was a physical manifestation of a sinful spiritual condition, and only the Messiah could truly take away sin. They also considered it impossible for someone who had been born blind to receive their sight.

Have you ever read the story in John 9 and asked yourself why the Pharisees and Sadducees in Jerusalem were so shocked? We read plenty of other accounts of Jesus healing blindness – what was the big deal with this one? It was the fact that the blind man was born blind and had never been able to see. There are even certain nuances within the text that suggest that there were no eyes in the sockets prior to Jesus bringing healing. That's what astonished them so. This was a sign of the Messiah, the creative miraculous ability to make those who were blind see. It is these Messiah miracles of Jesus that caused the people to marvel so much and the Pharisees to probe far more. It wasn't cynicism driving them; they were actually doing their job. They were supposed to test the people who claimed messiahship. For the most part they didn't bother, as those claiming to be the Messiah usually fell far short of the standard expected. It was not because of their lack of faith in Jesus that they tested him – on the contrary, it showed that they believed that he might just be the one they were looking for.

I heard a story recently of a group of tourists in Israel who happened upon an art exhibition and in the course of looking at the various masterpieces, came across a Jewish man who

128

had survived the Holocaust of Nazi Germany and expressed his emotions in powerful abstract art.

A lady from the group of tourists plucked up the courage to draw alongside him and speak to him. 'Excuse me, sir, I hope you don't mind me saying that I find your artwork very inspiring and moving.'

'Why, thank you,' replied the elderly man.

'Can I ask you which of your works is your favourite?'

The man turned to her with a gentle smile and replied 'Madam, are you married?'

'Erm … yes, yes I am,' she responded, slightly puzzled. 'Why do you ask?'

'And madam, do you have any children?' the man continued.

'Actually, yes, I have three children.' The confusion was growing in her voice. 'But why do you ask?' she replied, with a gentle shake of the head.

With a wry smile the man replied, 'My dear, which is your favourite?'

And with that the penny dropped. The lady left that place with the answer to her question, not simply because the artist responded, but because by asking her the questions he took her to an understanding that did not come to her through external influences but that was born within her.

Our Rabbi Jesus does the same. He is interested in taking us through the process so that we can come to an answer for ourselves. When we do, that answer cannot be taken away. So often we think of Jesus as the 'answer man' or that somehow as Christians we must hold all the answers. And yes Jesus is the answer, but he is more concerned about changing us than changing our circumstances.

I am sure that every person reading this book can tell me about times when you have cried out to God, poured out your heart to him, fallen on your knees in desperate prayer for an answer, only to hear God reply with what seems like a total curve ball. In the book of Job we go through over thirty excruciatingly painful chapters and round-about musings about the nature of God and Job voicing his utter desperation. Finally when we feel like giving up and skipping to something exciting like Acts 2, there's a storm, and not just any storm – this is a storm of epic proportions. Finally, after hearing Job and his friends talk and talk and talk, we now hear a different voice. The voice of Almighty God booms out from the trembling thunder and flashing lightning. Ah at last we think, finally we are going to get the answer, is Job right, are his friends right? Are they all wrong? Yahweh will now set us straight! Right? Well... kinda...

> Do you know when the mountain goats give birth?
> Do you watch when the doe bears her fawn? (v. 1)
> Who let the wild donkey go free? Who untied his ropes?
> (v. 5)

The Almighty is questioning the questioner. But what is God really doing here? Are these just random questions? Of course not! God has a purpose. He is showing his otherness, he is stating that he is far and above, majestic and powerful. Do we have an arm like God´s? Can our voice thunder like his? If he sees and controls all the deep and intricate ways of the universe, he can certainly look after us. The things Job feared came upon him, because he had a warped view of God. But now as he stood in the midst of the storm his eyes were opened. God questions us, offends our minds to reveal our hearts, and lets us walk on mountaintops and through deep valleys, ultimately so that we may know him and be known by him, but also that we may know his ways. Likewise, if I can bring you to a truth by questioning you it is no longer simply my truth, it becomes your truth, coming from within you and when it is your truth, not simply my truth – no one can take it from you.

The Rabbinical technique of teaching in this way is a very fine art and the response question is supposed to contain within its essence the answer. If you ever get the chance to observe in a *yeshiva* a Rabbi asking his *talmidim* (disciples) a question in this way, it is quite a sight to see them all begin to discuss, quote scriptures, quote Rabbis and share ideas with amazing depth and insight, all talking over one another, yet processing the overload of information with speed and clarity. It is very inspiring and humbling.

In Luke 20:1–8, Jesus is teaching in the Temple when the chief priests, scribes and elders come to question his authority. There is a fascinating aside here, in that scripture at the least infers that there were many people who also believed that John the Baptist had *shmicha*. They considered this other young, wild-eyed, long-haired (I like to think it was dreadlocked Rastafarian style – he was a Nazirite and so never cut his hair!) man to be an honoured Rabbi. Wow. No wonder the religious people were finding it tough to get their heads around all this. There is also wrapped up in the text the inference that Jesus may well have studied under John at some point. We can't prove that categorically but there are grounds for such a belief. At the very least Jesus is saying, 'John and I – our Rabbi is Yahweh!'

As we follow this Rabbi Jesus, we begin to realise that he believes in the untapped, unlimited potential within us and longs for us to allow him to draw it out from us. This is why, time and time again we see Jesus asking questions – he believes that the divine stamp is on us, that eternity is in our hearts. Somewhere deep within our spiritual DNA we know this to be true. We need to look inside ourselves – there we will find him and everything we need. And so, he continues to ask us the questions.

CHAPTER 9

DUST

Talmid is the Jewish word for disciple – to form the plural in Hebrew when the word is masculine you add '...im' to the end of it. So *talmidim* therefore means disciples. Only Rabbis with *shmicha* could have *talmidim*. A *talmid* is far more than simply a student – in our very western way of thinking, when we think of discipleship we often think of a teacher– student relationship, in which we gather information so that we may know what the teacher knows. How many Christian discipleship courses are there on the market that list subjects and end in a thesis? Don't get me wrong, there is great value in knowledge, understanding and formation in our walk with Christ, but this in and of itself is not discipleship. Whereas a student wants to know what his or her teacher knows to gain a diploma, certificate or degree, a *talmid* wants to be who their Rabbi is.

We cannot understand the twelve radicals that Jesus sent out into the world if we look at them through western eyes and see them as simply wanting to understand Jesus' teaching and pass it on. For Peter, James, John, their relationship with Jesus was so much more. They wanted

133

more than anything else to be just like their Rabbi, to eat like him, to talk like him, to love like him, to be bold and courageous like him and to suffer like him. You would not believe the passion that these guys had to be just like Jesus.

We find stories in the Mishnah of disciples following their Rabbis everywhere, hanging on their every word, to the extent that they would even follow them into the bathroom! That might make us laugh, but they wanted to know whether there was a blessing that their Rabbi would announce that they needed to also follow. As Jewish prayer is constant and covers every subject imaginable, there were indeed blessings that one was supposed to pronounce following visits to the bathroom. This is called the Asher Yatzer – 'He who formed mankind', and goes like this:

> Blessed are you, Hashem our God, King of the universe, who formed man with wisdom and created within him many openings and many hollows. It is obvious and known before your throne of glory that if even one of them ruptures, or if even one of them becomes blocked, it would be impossible to survive and to stand before you (even for a short period). Blessed are you, Hashem, who heals all flesh and acts wondrously.

If you think that's strange, you probably have never had the misfortune of one of those 'openings' or 'hollows' not working!

There were terms used to describe the *talmid*'s passionate pursuit of the Rabbi – one was to 'sit at a Rabbi's feet'. Acts 22:3 states that Paul had this type of *talmid* relationship with the great Rabbinic teacher Gamaliel. Mary the sister of Martha was said to 'sit at the feet' of Jesus

(Luke 10:38–42). This was a radical statement indeed in the culture of Jesus' day, because he was in a very real sense accepting a woman as his disciple and saying that she could be just like him. No wonder Martha, who was following cultural norms, got so upset! The other term was to be in 'the dust of the Rabbi'. What was meant by this was that the *talmid* so desperately wanted to follow their Rabbi that the very dust that flicked up from their sandals was seen as precious and they wanted to be so close that the dust would cover them. They wanted to catch the fire in their Rabbi's heart. Perhaps this is one explanation for the phenomenon of gold dust appearing on followers around the world in recent times as they seek to be in the close intimate presence of Jesus. The streets of heaven are paved with gold after all!

Bearing all of this in mind, we also need to realise the radical nature of the Rabbinic call 'Follow me'. When a Rabbi said to someone, 'Follow me', they didn't simply mean, 'Come with me or be a part of my team'. In effect what they were saying was. 'I believe that you can be like me.' Jesus believes that we can be like him. Isn't that amazing! He believes that the works he did, we will do also, and even greater works.

 The young Jewish girl Anne Frank, who grew up in the horrors of the holocaust and who wrote perhaps the most famous diary of all time describing her family's two years in hiding during World War II wrote, 'Everyone has inside of him a piece of good news. The good news is that you don't know just how great you can be! How much you can love!

What you can accomplish! And what your potential is!' I am sure she never imagined how her words would go around the world for many generations after she was mercilessly silenced by the Nazis. Yet her voice lives on and her words need to be heard today.

Jesus believes we can walk on water, calm the storms, turn the other cheek and carry our cross. It was a glorious and liberating day in my life when I realised that even though I did not believe in myself, my Rabbi and Saviour Jesus Christ believed in me.

I was extraordinarily blessed to grow up in a family where love was central, Jesus was real and life was full of goodness. My parents were in love and loved us as a result, and their love came out of their deep relationship and commitment to God. It was a heady time during the new church movement in the UK – the house churches that had sprung up all over the country during the 1970s had now outgrown the living rooms and garages where God had been so present and were filling school and town halls with the same fire and passion. We had found a God who was not limited to stained glass windows or hymnals, great though those can be – a God whose wonders could be experienced without having to wait for an afterlife. We had found a Messiah with a movement, not an idol with an institution, and our hearts burned with a desire to see his kingdom of love, hope and justice revolutionise the earth.

The church community I grew up in believed passionately in the family as God's plan and children were valued very highly. As a result the network of churches that we belonged to hosted a wide variety of powerful children's ministries, two of which came out of our home church. From as young as I can remember I was exposed to the presence and power of God. We were encouraged to use the gifts of the Holy Spirit and it wasn't unusual to see healing on a regular basis. I'll never forget the youth camp, where my later great friend and mentor Rich Hubbard prayed for me to be 'filled with the Spirit'. The only way I can describe what happened is to say that it felt like a wave crashed into me and for the rest of that night I couldn't stop speaking in tongues and worshipping God.

Little did we know that our whole world was about to be hit by a different kind of wave. In 1986 my little sister Miriam came on the scene. I was six years old and very happy to have another little sister, but a short time after Miriam arrived my mum noticed lumps growing under her armpit and on her breast. The doctors initially thought it was likely to be a result of her breast milk, but sent her for some tests which confirmed the worst – they were cancerous tumours and she would immediately have to begin a course of radiotherapy and chemotherapy.

We watched my mum begin to lose her hair and lose weight as she battled with a monster trying to take her away from us. The doctors, while always working hard, gave little hope and one day, unknown to us kids, told Dad that Mum might only have six months left to live and at very best, with much treatment, eighteen months. Aside from prolonging the inevitable, they could not see any other possibilities for my mum. They told Dad to prepare himself and everyone for my mum's death.

One of my most vivid memories from that time is from that same evening or very shortly after. I found my dad sitting on the edge of his bed, guitar in hand. He was nearly always playing his guitar – he wrote and recorded family worship music for many years. We would often find him with tears streaming down his face as he worshipped his God and that day was no exception. These tears were different though. They didn't seem to be tears of hope, but tears of anguish. Even in my little six-year-old perception I could tell there was something very wrong. He put his guitar down on the bed and picked me up, sitting me on his knee and holding me tight.

'What's wrong, Dad?' I said. 'Please don't cry.' He looked at me and simply said in a choked voice, 'We may have to learn to live without your mum.' He continued to hold me close as I tried to grasp what that might mean. Perhaps he didn't realise it at the time but one word in that phrase that stuck in my head offered a glimmer of hope. It was the word 'may'. It turned out that this glimmer was enough for my mum to grab hold of and with incredible determination, she began to fight against the odds. She decided that the doctors did not have the last say – her creator, the maker of heaven and earth, the healer Jesus of Nazareth, who the scriptures say is the same yesterday, today and forever, could heal her.

She began to devour the Bible. Suddenly our house was plastered with my mum's homemade Post-It notes, with scripture after scripture pertaining to her situation. She was taking a medicine more powerful than any other. It was not only the walls that became home for these curious phrases out of the Bible – she would speak them out loud to herself all the time. We thought she'd gone crazy! My brother and I would be watching television when all of a sudden we would hear my mum bellow out in the adjacent kitchen, 'I WILL NOT DIE BUT LIVE, AND DECLARE WHAT THE LORD HAS DONE FOR ME!' We would giggle to ourselves back then, but now we understand that she was taking God's word like a sword and fighting against thoughts of defeat.

It was certainly a fierce battle. Once a complete stranger came and knocked on our front door and when my mum answered he began to shout obscenities and proclamations of death and hell over her! My mum, though shaken, immediately spoke truth and continued to fight. She was convinced that Jesus' sacrifice on the cross was for her physical healing, just as much as for her spiritual one. By his wounds she HAD been healed. As far as she was concerned her body just had to get in line with that higher truth. She would stare the monster down.

Six months came, six months went by. There was no trace of cancer in her body. She was a picture of health. She never even seemed to have a cold during that time. The doctors continued carrying out the tests and every time the results would be clear. They couldn't understand it, but nor could they deny it. That was twenty-five years ago and she is still a picture of health.

Seeing God's word not simply respected, but intentionally used and believed in has forever changed the way I live, study and believe. However it would soon be my turn to face my own monster and I wouldn't be so successful. When I was thirteen the church we attended went through an incredibly difficult and painful split. At the same time we lost loved ones in the family, my hormones were playing havoc with my world and emotionally I felt like I was riding the big dipper. As one does at this age, I began to question everything. I doubted my belief and believed my doubts, and even doubted my doubts in my beliefs – you get the picture.

It was the grunge revolution in the music scene of the

early 1990s and bands like Nirvana and Pearl Jam filled the airwaves, giving voice and vent to what the previous so-called 'Generation X' were so angry about. Their words resonated with a tuned-out youth and in my questioning and negativity I jumped on the boat, with no idea that there would be icebergs ahead. I distanced myself from church – it was all just a bit too painful – and in my distancing moved closer to crowds that didn't help me. One of my closest friend's parents were drug dealers in the seaside town I grew up in and so inevitably it was only a matter of time before we began to experiment. I hated myself for what I was doing and was petrified of my parents finding out, mainly because I knew how very disappointed they would be with me. The lies started to come thick and fast to cover my tracks.

I was also overweight as a kid and now at thirteen I was determined to lose the weight. I was a bully and I was bullied. I was really starting to despise myself and knew I had to do something about it. The problem was that I didn't know where to begin. I didn't know where to look and so I looked in all the wrong places. I started to exercise and work out at the gym like crazy. I would spend hours trying to shift the pounds, and then eat meagre amounts of food to placate the aching hunger in my belly. It wasn't long before the weight started to drop off. I was so pleased with myself at first, but it wasn't enough, I needed to achieve more. So I upped the exercise and limited my intake. I would constantly lie to my parents about eating at my friend's houses, or come up with some other fabrication. Before long I was going for very long periods of time not eating. Sooner or later the hunger would get the better of me and I would binge on something and then, horrified by my actions, would force myself to vomit out what I had eaten.

I believe my coffee addiction started to take root around here, as I would drink lots of strong black coffee to give me energy. Another, more destructive addiction also began to rear its ugly head. I was miserable, constantly hungry and couldn't understand why I wasn't happy. I began to drink heavily, at first with friends but before long, I was drinking alone. I tended to drink spirits because they would have a quick effect and I could get away with it for long periods of time, as my parents would only visit their drinks collection very rarely. However, there was a terrible moment on one occasion when my parents found a large bottle of Jack Daniels that I had emptied within a couple of days.

My body ached. My mind was full of lyrics by Kurt Cobain the lead singer of Nirvana. He was my idol and I wanted to be just like him, and as his journey towards self-destruction became ever more critical, so did mine. On 8 April 1994 Kurt Cobain was found dead in his home in Seattle, Washington with a gunshot wound to the head and a suicide note. It had a profound effect on me. I believed I would follow in his footsteps. I learnt guitar, absorbed teenage angst like a sponge, grew my hair long, bleached it blonde and wrote songs and poetry about death, depression and despair. No wonder I couldn't get a girlfriend back then!

For three gruelling years I battled with anorexia and bulimia, seeing psychiatrists and doctors regularly. My parents were a rock during this time and my amazingly supportive siblings, wider family and greater church community were locked in a fierce battle for my survival, while I for the most part just kept blindly walking towards the precipice. On a number of occasions I nearly took my life, often with one foot over the chasm before somehow, something pulled back. Deep down I knew death wasn't the end.

My weight dropped to 4 stone 9 pounds. I could count my ribs, my skin stretched tight around my cheeks; I was more skeleton than person. I would often pass out from exhaustion. I had to visit the famous Maudsley children's psychiatric hospital in London on a weekly basis. My amazing, supportive praying family put up with far more from me than they ever deserved. Even in my worst and most abusive moments, they continued to love me and believe that I would eventually overcome this giant. Mum, Dad, Ben, Beth and Miriam, I could never thank you enough for how you loved me and stood by me.

During this time in our home church there was a wonderful youth worship movement going on called Cutting Edge. In time the Cutting Edge band would go on to be known as Delirious?, and to be used by God to change, in many ways, the essence of contemporary Christian worship music. From time to time my very faithful and at this time, deeply concerned brother would drag me along. More often than not I would be overwhelmed by the presence of God in those meetings and would have to leave, not being able to handle it. At one of those Cutting Edge events a young Martin Smith and his wife Anna, who had been a family friend since I was very young, saw me wander in beneath the usual dark cloud of depression that hung around me. I looked ghostlike. Later I would find out that Martin turned to Anna and said, 'I am not going to let that boy die'. Along with many others they began to pray. In fact my brother somehow managed to drag me out of the house to pray with Martin once a week and it definitely started to sow seeds of hope in me that things could be different.

There was, however, one area of my rebellion which was positive. I arrived at a conclusion around two years into my struggle with anorexia that if I carried on with my group of friends, I would get nowhere. I rebelled against them and as a result never got into the heavy drugs that they were by then doing. I began to study hard and became a nerd. It was all part of my search for something to fill the void. Something had to make me feel happy, there had to be some way to stop the pain.

I finished my final GCSE exam and left for the short walk back to my home. I had given my all and knew that I had done well in my exams, so why did I feel so desperately low? I didn't know where else to turn and decided that I couldn't face another day. My mind was set, my emotions numb and calculated. I would end my life that day. I arrived back to my house and made my way to my room, a lethal concoction of pills at hand, and sat on the edge of my bed gazing into the emptiness of the enormity of what I was about to do. In desperation I decided to pray one last prayer.

God, I knew you once ...
But you seem so far away ...
I don't know how to get back to you.
I don't know if you would even want to take me back.

I know this isn't the end ...
I know you are real, even if I don't know anything else.

If you will have me, I'll give you what little is left of my
    life ...
I've shown what a complete mess I've made of it on
    my own...
But if you don't do anything, I can't go on.
I will end my life today.

What happened next is difficult to describe in words but somehow, something far greater than me filled my little bedroom, knocking me over. I was pinned to the floor face down, unable to move. I felt as if my spirit was leaving my body. I was petrified, but at the same time felt waves of love too wonderful to describe. There was an explosion of emotion that had been tightly bottled up within me, that suddenly I could no longer stop from being released. I was aware that I was sobbing.

As if in a dream I saw myself in a pit. It was dark and sinister, covered in weeds and loose crumbling, filthy mud. Every time I tried to climb out, I would slip back down, and with each fall the pit seemed to grow and become more unbearable. I finally gave up, head in hands, sobbing, when a hand reached in, grabbed hold of me and forcefully and painfully yanked me up and out of the pit. Then I remember looking at the face of the person who had pulled me out and somehow knowing that it was Jesus. I have never been able to explain or really define exact features, other than the amazing, piercing eyes. I remember having the sensation that they had seen everything, that they had cried my tears, watched me stumble, watched me make mistake after mistake and yet those eyes burned with utter, unconditional love and I felt both torn and healed, lost and found, dead, yet more alive than I had ever known.

Then he spoke to me in a voice, which was gentle, yet full of power and authority. He said, 'If you give me your life, I will take you on an adventure that will take your breath away, make the hairs on the back of your neck stand on end and leave you wondering how on earth you can live up to the amazing plans I have for you. I believe in you.'

When I finally came round, what had seemed like moments had been hours and though I couldn't even begin to comprehend what had happened to me, I knew my life was never going to be the same again. I quickly phoned my mum and dad, then my granddad, who came over to the house to be with me. I couldn't explain what had just happened, I just knew through my tears of excitement that something had changed, that I didn't feel the same. I remember finding a piece of scrap paper and writing out a kind of declaration of faith that from now on things would be different. My mum still keeps that scrap of paper in her bedside cabinet.

From that day things would never be the same again. Any desire to lose myself in drugs or alcohol left me completely, and though my relationship with food didn't change overnight, the journey had certainly begun. American actor and writer George Carlin once said, 'Just 'cause you've got the monkey off your back, it doesn't mean the circus has left town.' There would still be a fight ahead. But there was an immediate sense of victory over this monster that had controlled me for so long. My head had been a receptacle for all kinds of lies and rubbish for three years and I was suddenly, desperately hungry to fill it with a new kind of food.

God's word and presence became my new addiction. I couldn't get enough. In every spare moment I would devour scripture and get lost in God's presence. I was changing from the inside out. Romans 12:2 says, 'Do not conform to the pattern of this world, but be transformed by the renewing of your mind.' My mind was essentially being made new. I am very pleased to say that I had been brainwashed by the Spirit of God. I no longer hated myself, nor wanted to die.

Life had become technicolour where once it had been grey and I desperately wanted to share this treasure I had found with everyone.

I had met with the Rabbi. He had said 'Follow me'. And just as he promised on that day in May 1997, he has taken me on a journey that has taken my breath away and made the hairs on the back of my neck stand on end. I still stand in awe at what he daily believes that I can be. There is nothing greater in life than to be a disciple of this Rabbi. He believes that we can be world-changers and history-makers. He believes that if we can grab hold of what he grabbed hold of, we could quite literally turn the world upside down. He believes that about you and me.

CHAPTER 10

FOLLOW

In Jesus' day to become a disciple of a Rabbi was no easy thing. It has been said that approximately one in every thousand actually achieved their dream, and to do so there was a long and arduous road to follow. Firstly they would have to start their journey in the Jewish schooling system that everyone had to attend.

Bet Sefer

Bet Sefer means 'the house of the book' and it was the first step of education. You would think that this might be a nice gentle entrance into the world of learning, like our kindergartens and infant schools. How many of you still have fond memories of those days, making plasticine models, playing in the sand pit, playing kiss chase during the morning break? Not so for these young hopefuls. At around six years old, a Jewish boy would go to a local synagogue school to start studying at this level until approximately the age of ten. These schools of learning are believed to have been established as early as the days of Ezra.

They would attend *Bet Sefer* from Monday to Friday.

Here the Torah teachers would be in their element, teaching the young bright-eyed boys the scriptures, specifically the Torah. As mentioned previously, Torah means 'guide' and can be used to refer to the entire Hebrew canon. However, in this instance we are referring to the first five books of the Hebrew Scriptures: Genesis, Exodus, Leviticus, Numbers and Deuteronomy.

There was said to be a tradition that went back to ancient times that on the first day of school the Rabbi or head Torah teacher would take a small piece of paper, sometimes rice paper, with the Shema prayer written on it and then smother it with honey and then proceed to encourage his young students to eat 'the word of God'. The Rabbi would say 'Never forget, that's what Adonai tastes like – may his word be like honey on your lips and water to your soul!' In effect he was saying, 'May the words of God be the most pleasurable, the most enjoyable thing you could ever comprehend and may that sweetness fill you with his presence.'

However, it was not all sticky, tasty exercises. Between the ages of six and ten they would have to memorise Genesis, Exodus, Leviticus, Numbers and Deuteronomy. Suddenly the ability to quote Psalm 23 seems rather paltry, doesn't it? Also it wasn't enough simply to be able to quote the scriptures – they were also required to be like a walking concordance. If the Torah teacher were to ask a young student, 'Where are the scriptures that refer to doves?', not only would the student have to be able to quote the scriptures, but he would also have to be able to say where to find them and explain the context in which they were placed. Needless to say, you had to be a brilliant student to achieve graduation from *Bet Sefer* and so the vast majority stopped here. If they didn't make the grade they went on to work in their father's business and to learn a trade.

Bet Talmud

The cream of the crop went on to what was known as *Bet Talmud* or 'the house of learning'. The age range for this school varied somewhat and does not seem to have ever been set in stone but was roughly from the ages of ten to fourteen. In *Bet Talmud*, the student would have to memorise the remaining Hebrew Scriptures all the way to Malachi. If we were to do that in English we would be talking about 46 books, 1074 chapters, 27,570 verses – 773,682 words in total. Deep breath! OK? By the age of thirteen or fourteen, these highly dedicated students would have the entire Hebrew text memorised. Even today in Jewish *yeshiva* seminaries they still do this. There is much work for us to do in the Christian church.

At this age the students would also begin learning the Jewish art of questioning. In our western schooling we are mainly encouraged to memorise information that we need to store to be able to complete tests and exams. But in Jesus' day, as mentioned previously, you would answer the question with a question. It is interesting to look at the pre-adolescent Jesus in the Temple at the age of twelve: 'They found him in the Temple, sitting in the midst of the teachers, both listening to them and asking them questions. And all who heard him were astonished at his understanding and answers' (Mark 2:46). When it came to scripture, Jesus was the best of the best. He knew how to answer with questions. Could it be that Jesus was rocking his way through *Bet Talmud*? What we can once again be sure of is that the vast majority of people never made it through to this stage and many of those who did simply had to drop out due to the pressure before making it to graduation. Once again the majority would now dedicate themselves to the family business.

Bet Midrash

Toward the end of studying at *Bet Talmud*, at around the ages of thirteen or fourteen years old, the very best of the best would go on to present themselves to a well-known respected Rabbi. The norm would be for these hopefuls to approach the Rabbi and to say something along the lines of, 'Rabbi, can I follow you? I want to become your disciple, your *talmid*, your student. Please let me be in your *Bet Midrash*, your house of study.' This tentative first encounter with their chosen Rabbi was just the beginning of a more arduous process and many, many questions. It was imperative for the Rabbi to find out if you were indeed the best of the best or not. The Rabbi had to be sure this individual had the potential to become just like him. He needed to know if the student followed his thinking, philosophy – what the Rabbis termed their 'yoke'. The questioning was intense and ongoing and would test the boy's scriptural knowledge, interpretation and ability to 'bind and loose', another Rabbinic term used to describe the formation of doctrine in line with the Rabbi's doctrine.

If you ever have a chance to see disciples testing their Rabbi's yoke, it is definitely worth taking the time to observe. Generally the disciple will come with a question such as 'Rabbi, what is the greatest commandment?' The Rabbi will respond with a question and the hum of conversation will begin, buzzing backward and forward and growing in intensity. Scriptures and quotes from the Mishnah and other ideas will fly about, and eventually they will come back with a question to answer the question. The game will grow in intensity and depth as the disciples come to a deeper realisation and revelation of what the Rabbi really thinks and feels. Now place the radical nature of Jesus' statement in Matthew 11:28 into that context.

> Come unto me, all you who are heavy laden, and I will give you rest. Take my yoke upon you and learn from me, for I am gentle and lowly in heart, and you will find rest for your souls. For my yoke is easy and my burden is light.

I used to think that this was a scripture referring to people burdened with sin or dragged down with problems. But that isn't what Jesus is saying. This is a scripture for the hair-splitting legalist, whose shoulders are burdened with theological theory and doctrinal dependence.

What was Jesus' yoke? In its essence it was simply this, to love the Lord your God with all your heart, soul and strength and to love your neighbour as yourself. Easy? Perhaps to learn and understand, but certainly not easy to live. It takes the power of the Holy Spirit. Christianity isn't difficult, it's impossible! Have you ever tried to love your neighbour as yourself? And Jesus even goes so far as to say we must love our enemies. If that wasn't bad enough, it's likely that he will use our 'loving our enemy' to actually get them saved and then we'll have to spend eternity with the rotters!

I am of course joking and want everyone to come into a relationship with God but we all know that this yoke is not very easy. We must love the unlovely, be kind to the cruel, and be selfless with the downright smelly! Without total dependence on our Rabbi and his presence within us, we could do nothing. The good news is that he is with us. He will never leave us or forsake us and even when we do not believe in ourselves, he believes in us.

In Jesus' day, if the Rabbi believed that you were the best of the best, that you were able to become like him, he would say, '*Lech acharai*' – 'Come, follow me.' To obey his call you would have to leave your family, your home, your village and the local synagogue where you had studied from the age of six. You would leave everything you had known, loved and been comfortable with to follow the Rabbi. This was the new life of a true *talmid*. It would cost you everything to become a disciple. From now on you would eat like your Rabbi, sleep and rise as your Rabbi would, speak and act like your Rabbi and learn and study Torah following the yoke of your Rabbi. From now on you would understand Yahweh as your Rabbi understood him.

Of course for many excellent, remarkable students when it came to being 'tested' by the Rabbi, they failed and the Rabbi would not invite them to follow him. He would encourage them to go home to their village, marry and have children and learn their family business. Those who failed were often heartbroken, but they knew that the Rabbis were the elite and despite their hardest efforts, they simply would not be good enough.

Jesus did help his father in his business, but thirteen times in the New Testament, Jesus is called a Rabbi (in Matthew 26:25, 49, Mark 9:5, 11:21 and 14:45 and John 1:38, 49, 3:2, 26, 4:31, 6:25, 9:2 and 11:8.) He is also called a teacher forty-one times. Only once is he called a carpenter (Mark 6:3), although the Greek word *tekton* is better translated as a stone mason or builder, or even an architect. But we see him dedicating his time and energy to raising a different type of building, made with living stones. He would raise up a future generation who would take his movement to the ends of the earth.

We see Jesus turn the process of selecting disciples entirely on its head. It would appear that those he called had almost certainly failed at best the *ip-hak shiham* or Rabbi test, but it's more likely that they were those who dropped out after *Bet Sefer*. To quote the band Switchfoot, Jesus chooses the church of 'the losers, the dropouts, the sinners, the failures and the thieves'. These weren't the elite, the learned and qualified. In Jewish religious circles they were nobodies. Bear this in mind when you see the astonishment of the Pharisees and Sadducees at the power of delivery and articulate teaching that Peter, the fisherman displays in the Jerusalem Sanhedrin.

This remarkable Rabbi Yeshua, who, if we follow the chronology of John's Gospel, has already done astonishing miracles said to be signs of the Messiah, wanders along a quiet Galilee coastline and meets two fisherman casting a net into the lake. He says to them, 'Come, follow me, and I will make you fishers of men.' They leave everything and follow him. I once heard a preacher talking about how that must have been a tough choice – why would they want to leave their successful business? Are you kidding me? They threw down those nets and ran after Jesus. This was the opportunity of a lifetime. They thought to themselves, 'How can this be? I'm a nobody, I've never achieved *Bet Talmud*, why does Jesus want me? And yet here he is, this worker of miracles, raiser of the dead and he is saying that I can be like him. He believes in me!'

So we find this impetuous, brash, loud, open ya mouth and stick your foot in it fisherman Peter, quite likely the oldest, always the one to speak or act first and think later. He's followed Jesus for some time now, seen him do amazing things, been used to do some pretty spectacular things himself. He is starting to believe, 'Maybe this Rabbi is right and I can be like him'. And then Jesus comes to them while they are in a boat on the lake in the middle of the night, walking on the water.

In the Jewish mindset the sea was often seen as the abyss, the place of the dead and the entrance to the shadowy underworld, Sheol. So it wasn't a surprise that they thought this was a visiting spirit. But Peter's statement 'If it is you, tell me to come to you on the water' is very telling when we understand the Jewish context. He's saying, 'You believe I can be like you and if you tell me that I can do it, I can do it. I will step out of this boat. I will risk failure, ridicule, even death, because I want to be just like my Rabbi. If you walk on water I want to walk on water too. You believe I can do it, right? Tell me to come!'

How many of us have walked on water? When I was little I tried it at the swimming pool and while paddling in the icy waters of the English channel, unfortunately to no avail! How much more of a big deal would it have been if there was a wind raging?

I'll never forget being in a P&O ferry travelling back from France to the UK. The year was 1987 and in October that year we faced the most serious hurricane the nation had seen, but even though things would get worse, that night on those rough waters, everyone was tense. The waters rose up above the small cabin windows and the huge hulk of a ship swayed backwards and forwards, up and down with relentless ebbs and sways, shaking everyone to the core and causing their stomachs to turn. The skies looked menacing and foreboding. It was scary.

Many years later I had the opportunity to sail across the sea of Galilee and my grandfather explained to me that the previous time he had been in the middle of the sea a wind came out of nowhere and the little fishing boat was tossed about and shaken. The curious thing, my grandfather noted, was that the waters had been calm and the skies clear when they set sail. Sounds like life, right? Ever felt like the skies are bright, the waters still and then out of the blue you are suddenly in the eye of a storm? The last thing you feel like doing in those moments is stepping out, or taking risks. Our human nature wants our doors and windows bolted up. But Peter gets out of the boat. How many times has Jesus asked us to get out of our boat, our comfort zone in the middle of a storm and come to him? To allow his power to cause us to walk all over what the enemy meant for our harm?

You might be facing all kinds of impossible and threatening situations right now: a serious illness, a loved one spiralling out of control, a business falling apart. It looks scary, it looks dark, everything in you wants to crawl up in a corner or hide under the blankets, and yet the miracle maker is not drowning under the situation. He's not fretting or breaking out into a cold sweat. He's on top of things, he's calm, and he's in control. You've seen him stop the storms before and wonder and hope that he will do that again. That he will wave his hand, say, 'Peace, be still' and it'll be all right. But Jesus doesn't try to make it any easier for Peter. He could have at least let the sun come out and the waves die down and then invite him out for a stroll. For some reason God loves to get us out of our comfort zones during the scariest opportunities. And out Peter got. He was a fisherman, he was in his zone, his world, and Jesus was saying 'Get out, you don't have to be held back, you don't have to be limited. I BELIEVE IN YOU! YOU CAN BE JUST LIKE ME!' That's why Peter got out – a revelation soared through his soul that he didn't have to wait for Jesus to 'do the stuff'. Christ in him the hope of the glory of God was sufficient for him to 'do the stuff'.

Ephesians 3:20 says, 'Now to him who is able to do immeasurably more than all we ask or imagine, according to his power that is at work within us.' The New King James Version says, 'exceedingly, abundantly, beyond', in the Greek '*huper, perissos, huper'*. Our word 'hyper' is derived from *huper*. It means above, beyond, more than, superseding 'super'. I remember staring in awe at the sheer size of a hypermarket in the south of France during a camping holiday in the mid-1980s. They were more than, above and beyond! *Perissos* means to be superior to, extraordinary, surpassing, uncommon. Then *huper* is repeated again. Paul is trying to make a ludicrously large, bounding, explosive statement of the awesomeness of God at work in us. You might have some amazingly big and scary dreams and thoughts, but I can assure based on the authority of Paul's statement that whatever you could think or imagine, God has something bigger.

The Irish writer and playwright George Bernard Shaw said, 'You see things; and you say "Why?" But I dream things that never were, and I say "Why not?"' We must become dreamers of the impossible and pull into today the dreams of tomorrow. You might have raised your dreaming to the level of supermarket thinking but Jesus is saying it's time for hypermarket thinking! Peter didn't think he could step out on the water because he was somehow more special than the others, but he did get this one thing settled in his heart – if his Rabbi could do it, he would follow him, not in his own strength but 'according to HIS power that is at work in us'. He climbed out of the boat.

Yes, he stumbled, lost focus and began to fall, and yes, Jesus rebuked him. 'Where is your faith, Peter?' However, I think we tend to completely miss the essence of this rebuke. Jesus wasn't saying 'Why don't you trust me, Peter?' Peter didn't doubt Jesus for one second. Peter doubted himself. Jesus is making a profound statement, saying 'Why don't you believe in yourself, Peter? I believe in you, I am with you and I've got your back, brother.'

It may come as somewhat of a surprise to you to read this today, but Jesus believes in you. He knows that there is incredible untapped potential within each one of us. God has an awesome plan and purpose for us that if he were to reveal it all to us would take our breath away. He believes in you! He believes in me! Jesus wants to be our Rabbi, our teacher, our master. He wants us to truly be his disciples, his students, his *talmidim*. He is calling us today, 'Come, follow me.' It doesn't matter who we are, how young or old we are, where we've been, what we have or have not accomplished or done with our lives. It is not reserved for the elite. It is not about how much you know – it is about *who* you know. If you know him and his call to follow, you can be assured that he believes that you can be like him. If he can lay hands on the sick and see them recover, he believes you can – if he can raise the dead, he believes

157

you can too. Nothing is impossible if we would just believe what he believes about us. This has huge ramifications for our understanding of the New Testament text.

In this culture a Rabbi's *talmidim* were generally around the age of fifteen and would study with the Rabbi, usually finding a bride at around the age of twenty and continuing their theological preparation. So why in the world do we see painting after painting of the disciples as elderly guys with beards? They would have been what we call adolescents today. Some even argue that a rendering of a Greek word used by the apostle John to describe himself in the Gospel of the same name as possibly referring to a pre-adolescent. Just think about this for a moment. Does it not radically force us to redefine the way we see not only the Gospel narratives but the very essence of kingdom expansion itself?

The first time I heard this theory it was from the Jerusalem School of Synoptic Research, which is a think-tank made up of Jewish and Christian scholars dedicated to better understanding the Synoptic Gospels. A shaft of revelation hit me and in many ways I'm still left reeling from it even now. First of all, the jigsaw pieces started to drop into position. I felt a huge burden lift. How many times had I read some of the narratives and thought, in a moment's arrogance, how could those disciples have been so immature? Obviously when we take a step back from the story, we realise that we are just as susceptible to the mistakes they made. However if we see those twelve as adolescent cheeky monkeys (I wonder if anyone else has referred to the twelve apostles as 'cheeky monkeys' before?) we can begin to understand some of their thoughts and actions. To place them as adolescents increases their reputation, and encourages and inspires me greatly.

As a little aside we must remember that in Jewish culture the age of thirteen is seen as the entrance into adulthood. According to Jewish law at the age of thirteen a Jewish boy or girl becomes responsible for their own actions. This age, it is believed, was chosen as naturally this is the age that most begin puberty. Today they hold a *Bar Mitzvah* (for males), or *Bat Mitzvah* (for females) ceremony which symbolises coming of age. *Bar Mitzvah* and *Bat Mitzvah* mean 'son of the law' and 'daughter of the law' respectively.

Whoever becomes *Bar* or *Bat Mitzvah* has the responsibilities of an adult Jew, under Jewish Law. These include:

- moral responsibility for one's own actions
- eligibility to be called to read from the Torah and participate in a *Minyan* (gathering). (In Orthodox denominations, only males read from the Torah or participate in a *Minyan*)
- eligibility to possess personal property
- eligibility to be legally married according to Jewish law
- a requirement to follow the 613 laws of the Torah and keep the Halakha

They were seen as adults, part of the community – they could marry, start businesses, and grow a beard, if they were able (I'm thirty-four at the time of writing and doubt I can!)

As you can probably tell, I not only like the idea of them being in this age bracket, but believe that the Jerusalem

School of Synoptic Research, and many other highly respected Christian and Jewish scholars are right. But what is the evidence for this theory?

The Pros for a Young Age

The Temple Tax
In Exodus 30:14–15, Jewish law states that every male over the age of twenty is to pay a half-shekel as a census offering when they visit the Temple of Yahweh. In Matthew 17:24–27, when the ever impetuous Peter asks Jesus concerning this issue, Jesus tells him to go and do what he's good at and to 'fish up' this tax. See the faith of this young man as he looks in the mouth of a slippery, flipping, flopping fish and finds the coins he needs. Jesus only seems to miraculously provide enough to pay the tax for two men, Peter and himself. Why? Could we conclude that the others were under age and did not need to pay?

The Use of the Term 'Little Ones'
In Matthew 11:25, Luke 10:21, and John 13:33, Jesus calls his disciples little children; a bit insulting, or even downright strange if they were peers.

They Were Unmarried
We know that Peter had a wife, as Jesus healed his mother-in-law (Matthew 8:14–15) but in the biblical narratives no other disciples' wives are mentioned. In those times a Jewish man could marry or at least legally be engaged from the age of thirteen but generally received his wife after the age of eighteen. For this you could deduce, though not

prove, that the disciples were unmarried and most probably under the age of eighteen.

The Education System of Israel at the Time of Jesus

In Avot 5 from the Mishnah, we learn of the ancient Jewish education traditions that we have already mentioned in detail. Jewish children began intensive study at young ages, but education for most concluded by the age of fifteen. For the 'best of the best' we have already mentioned, higher education consisted of studying under a local Rabbi, and if they were distinguished, they could begin teaching as a Torah teacher once they reached the age of thirty. If at fifteen students were not accepted by a Rabbi, they then entered the workforce. The disciples tended to be working at their fathers' trades, most likely having been rejected from formal education by other Rabbis.

In the light of all that we have learnt from Rabbinic tradition and advances in historical and Jewish Second-Temple era cultural studies, to place the disciples as older simply doesn't make sense in the world in which Jesus lived. A man over thirty leaving his trade to follow a Rabbi would be totally counter-cultural, although obviously not impossible (Jesus was definitely counter-cultural), but it seems more likely that they were younger rather than older.

The Zeal and Folly of Youth

The behaviour of the disciples, as detailed in the Gospels, fits well with the zealous nature and foolishness of adolescence. Doesn't it make more sense that teenagers, rather than grown men, were arguing over who would be greatest in Jesus' kingdom? Picture a gang of teenagers instead of work-hardened men in the boat when the storm hit, fear-stricken and waking up Jesus for help. The forgetful and distracted nature of youth helps me understand how they could hear Jesus say he would die and come back to life over and over again and yet act as they did when these things did actually take place. They were kids. They hadn't been paying attention in class, they had been checking out the cute girls at that particular moment!

What we do see that gives us hope is that they were quick to admit their failures, and showed they had limitless amounts of energy in storming the country with the good news of Messiah. They were radical, free of weights of responsibility, still naive enough to believe that anything was possible. Age and disappointment wouldn't hold them back. They did go and turn the world upside down, and if church tradition can be trusted on estimated times of their martyrdom, then a younger age also makes sense as if we place them as older men they would have lived to be, well, ancient!

The Cons for a Young Age

I do need to be balanced and weigh up the potential cons of this theory, as I'm sure there are many who will still find this quite hard to swallow, so let's take a journey into the arguments against and see whether they help or hinder our case.

Matthew Was a Tax Collector

The Bible doesn't say Matthew was apprenticed to be a tax collector, or that his father was a tax collector, but that Matthew himself was a Roman appointed tax agent.

Would the Romans have trusted a teenager with this job? Again we have to view this in light of the culture – teenagers were considered adults and we are not talking about gathering taxes using advanced systems. Gathering tax from a fishing business could mean that that business gave you ten out of every hundred fish caught. You didn't need an advanced degree in accounting to accomplish that! We also know that tax collectors worked in little Mafia-like groups. They were considered very sinful not only because of their reputation for stealing, but because of the company they kept, the parties they held and the loose women their money could pay for. What more could a teenage dropout in Galilee want?

Jesus Entrusted His Mother to the Disciple John

At the cross, Jesus entrusts the care of his mother to John. This is a very strange passage because we know that Jesus had younger brothers. Should it not have been their responsibility to look after their mum? At this point, if you take the young age view, John could have been as young as thirteen. Would Jesus have trusted someone so young for this task? You could argue that Jesus knew John would outlive all the others, and according to church tradition, he did, so he was the most reliable choice. Reading the Gospels we see that James, John and Peter were Jesus' inner circle. Jesus knew Peter was married and had a mother-in-law to look after. He must have known that James would give his life as a martyr a number of years later, so John again was the sensible choice. Jesus was also close to John and may have recognised that he could handle this responsibility. I think of the young pioneers in the early settling of the American West who were entrusted the care of their families at very young ages. Age may not have mattered to Jesus, but it's worth considering.

Does It Really Matter?

It very much depends on how you view the narrative and flow of events in the New Testament era. It's impossible to say one way or another what age the disciples were, and since the Bible doesn't make a big deal of it, perhaps neither should we. I like the idea of a younger age for the disciples, firstly because it appeals to my common sense. However, I also like the idea because God wants to touch our lives, set us on fire and move us into destinies beyond our wildest dreams. I believe he wants to do this in our lives before we fall into the lie that grows so often as we move past our age of innocence and nest of naivety, that we're just not good enough, fast enough and clever enough. When we were young, we believed we could take on the world, we were passionate about everything. Can you imagine what would happen if we tapped into this passion of youth and got our young people blazing a trail for Jesus before anyone told them they couldn't? They could change the world!

The American general Douglas MacArthur once lamented,

> People grow old only by deserting their ideals. Years may wrinkle the skin, but to give up interest wrinkles the soul. You are as young as your faith, as old as your doubts, as young as your confidence, as old as your fear, as young as your hope, as old as your despair. In the central place of every heart there is a recording chamber. So long as it receives messages of beauty,

hope, cheer and courage, so long are you young. When you heart is covered by the snow of pessimism and the ice of cynicism, then and then only are you grown old. And then, indeed as the ballad says, you just fade away.

The scriptures say that those who wait on the Lord will renew their strength – they will mount up like eagles, run and not grow weary, walk and not faint. Psalm 103 says, 'He fills our mouths with good things so that our youth is renewed like the eagle's.' God wants young, vibrant hearts on fire, no matter what our physical age. We are never too old to become young again.

Second Chance

Something else that we note about this Rabbi and his relationship with his *talmidim* is that Jesus was like no other Rabbi in his love and acceptance even in the face of their huge errors and failings. Peter, the waltzer of the waters, the stomper of the seas, blurts out in the Passover meal, 'Jesus, I'll never fail you, I'll never let you down.' Jesus turns to him and says 'You know, Peter, before the cockerel crows three times you'll disown me.' To deny or disown your Rabbi was a grave and most dishonouring thing to do. Not only would you be excommunicated from his school of learning and *Minyan*, but it was extremely unlikely that any other Rabbi would ever consider taking you under his wing. I'm sure Peter was both horrified and deeply saddened that Jesus considered that he could disown him. 'After all we've been through, Jesus? How could you think that of me?' Yet sure enough, just a few short hours later, this dedicated warrior, riled by a servant girl's taunts, buckles under the intensity of the pressure. 'I swear I do not know him!' I wonder if those words choked him slightly as they left his lips, that night in Jerusalem.

The scriptures say that Jesus simply turned to look at him. Now beaten, bloodied and broken-hearted, his eyes that pierced like bolts of lightning locked with Peter's in both intensity and love, and Peter wept bitterly. He thought there was no way back. He knew the culture – he realised what he had done. He might as well go back to fishing because he was finished as a follower of Jesus.

But this Rabbi is different. Once Jesus has risen from the dead, he doesn't wait for Peter to go to him, he actually seeks him out and desires to restore him back into his heart and into his inner circle. In John 21 we read that early one morning he is waiting for the disciples on the shore when they return from a night's unsuccessful fishing. Having instructed them to throw their net on the other side of the boat, resulting in a miraculous haul of fish, he is cooking breakfast for them when they return.

I can imagine the tension and the rollercoaster of emotions going on inside Peter at this meeting. Will Jesus rebuke him? Will he forgive him? Shame and excitement must have been burning within him. When they have finished eating, Jesus turns to him and there is the following:

'Simon son of John, do you love me more than these?'
'Yes, Lord,' he said, 'you know that I love you.'
Jesus said, 'Feed my lambs.'
Again Jesus said, 'Simon son of John, do you love me?'
He answered, 'Yes, Lord, you know that I love you.'
Jesus said, 'Take care of my sheep.'

> The third time he said to him, 'Simon son of John, do
>   you love me?'
> Peter was hurt because Jesus asked him the third time,
> 'Do you love me?' He said, 'Lord, you know all things;
>   you know that I love you.'
> Jesus said, 'Feed my sheep.'

Much has been said about these verses and the significance
of the Greek word used here. Jesus first of all, asks Peter,
twice, if he loves him, using the Greek word *phileo*, to which
Peter responds that Jesus knows he *phileo* loves him, but
then Jesus uses a different Greek word, *agape,* but Peter is
only able to respond with *phileo. Phileo* means, according
to Strong's concordance:

1. to love
    a. to approve of
    b. to like
    c. to sanction
    d. to treat affectionately or kindly, to welcome, befriend
2. to show signs of love to
3. to be fond of

This kind of word for love was very strong and enduring, it
was the word used for the bond of love within a family. It
wasn't a weak love, as many have suggested. It spoke of
commitment, endurance and covenant relationship. *Agape*
on the other hand is identified as 'to love dearly, with
an intense commitment'. *Agape* is the kind of love Paul
describes in 1 Corinthians 13: '*Agape* is patient, *agape* is
kind. It does not envy, it does not boast, it is not proud. It
does not dishonour others, it is not self-seeking, it is not

easily angered, it keeps no record of wrongs. *Agape* does not delight in evil but rejoices with the truth. It always protects, always trusts, always hopes, always perseveres. *Agape* never fails.'

Many would say that Peter has come to a realisation of his own frailty, and while by faith he may wish to say that he loves Jesus with that full commitment, he knows firsthand the sting of disappointment with himself, and he's not about to blurt out his willingness to follow Jesus to the death again. Ironically it is in his very admission of his inability to do so that prompts Jesus to make a rather cryptic statement suggesting that Peter would indeed stand strong even to his death and that he would not fail him again.

Knowing my bent towards all things Jewish and my firm belief that at the very least the New Testament was passed orally in the Hebrew language, we must be careful to not be too dogmatic in our interpretations of the text here. In Hebrew thinking repetition is very significant. There isn't really a way to describe progression or intensity as we know it. For instance there isn't a way to say 'good, better, best'. Instead the level is intensified by repetition. Good = good / good, good = better / good, good, good = best. In Isaiah's amazing encounter with God in Isaiah 6, the seraphim declaring, 'Holy, holy, holy is the Lord Almighty' are making a statement about the intensity of the holiness of God.

Jesus doesn't ask Peter his question three times because he keeps forgetting his answer. He asks him three times to find out about the intensity of his love and commitment. Peter denied Jesus three times. Jesus wanted to reverse this, and for Peter to make a thorough recommitment.

Can you imagine this moment? Peter's heart leaps with joy at the fact that his Rabbi stands before him alive, and he's not there disciplining, criticising and dragging Peter down. Rather, he has those same arms that were wide open stretched and nailed to a cross, now wide open to accept him in an embrace. He is not turning his back on this failed *talmid* – he is giving him an awesome mission.

Jesus says to Peter, 'Feed my sheep', 'Feed my lambs'. He is placing Peter in the profession of a shepherd. In the Old Testament the figure of the shepherd always referred first of all to God ('The Lord is my shepherd'), then secondly to the rulers of Israel. Jesus is comparing Peter to the loving, caring, providing heavenly Father and bestowing a royal crown on his head. He is saying in effect, 'I have not given up on you, Peter. I still believe that you can be just like me. Put your shoulders back, lift up your head. You are my son. Believe again, Peter! Your stumbling blocks will be your stepping stones; I will make your setbacks into something glorious. Feed my lambs – be like me. Feed my sheep – be like me. I believe in you.'

Peter messed up, you and I have messed up, but God wants to take our mess and make a message out of it. He gives us test after test so that we may have a testimony. I may fail him a thousand times, both outwardly in actions that don't reflect those of my Rabbi and inwardly as I think and feel out of this jar of clay and earth. But he will never say that he is through with us. This potter will keep working the clay, keep believing, not simply that we will be a masterpiece one day, but actually that we are already masterpieces, we are his workmanship, his poetry in motion. This Rabbi will never stop reaching out and saying to us that he believes that we can be like him.

169

Can you hear him? The voice of your father, the voice of many waters that sounds like a trumpet? He's crying out to you, saying, 'Come up here, come up higher, come closer. Be covered in the dust of the Rabbi. You are my beloved. Come and look into my eyes that blaze like fire, hear me speak over you, sing over you, declare over you that I am for you, not against you. I am yours and you are mine. It doesn't matter how far you have fallen, if you've squandered everything, ended up in the pig sty wanting to fill your belly with pig swill. If you have denied me and slapped me on the face, I turn my other cheek to you. I love you, I believe in you, I'm waiting for you to believe me. When you believe me, you can become all I say you can be, accomplish every dream, overcome every obstacle and defeat every enemy. Come my son, my daughter, do you love me? Be like me!'

CHAPTER 11

LIGHTS OF THE WORLD

Caesarea Philippi was an ancient Roman city located at the southwestern base of Mount Hermon. The city is mentioned in the Gospels on a number of occasions, and was located within the region known as the *Panion*, named after the Greek god Pan, who was associated with the grotto and shrines close to the spring called Paneas. Today the city, now no longer inhabited, is an archaeological site located within the Golan Heights.

 In Greek mythology the satyrs are deities of the woods and mountains. They are usually depicted as being half human and half beast – they tend to have goats' tails, flanks and hooves, while the upper parts of their bodies are human. They also have goats' horns. They were usually companions of Dionysus, who depending on who you ask, was really the god of orgies and drunkenness. They spent their time getting wasted, dancing and chasing nymphs!

Pan had a wrinkled face and a prominent pointy

chin. On his forehead were two horns and he had a hairy body. According to mythology he was a swift runner and able to climb rocky ledges with ease. Pan belonged to Dionysus' entourage and in many ways exceeded him in his insatiable appetites and lusts. As such he was not particularly well liked by the other gods and was looked down upon, as were the majority of fertility gods.

In dualistic Greek thinking everything was black and white, pure or defiled. Pan displayed unbridled male sexuality and carnal desire. In the form of a goat he constantly chased nymphs through the forest. As such, rape became almost an act of worship for followers of Pan. The word 'panic' used in everyday modern English has its roots in the irrational fear that young ladies were known to have when walking through solitary places, thinking Pan might be hot on their trail.

Originally Caesarea Philippi was the area dedicated to Baal and Asherah worship. It was the red light district, the seediest, darkest area in the so called 'Holy' Land. When Alexander the Great arrived on his mission of Hellenisation, he very astutely decided that, rather than suppressing the current beliefs, he would replace them with his Hellenistic beliefs. Many forms of syncretised religions formed, combining facets of Hellenism with the current local beliefs and bringing about a much quicker assimilation into the culture. These curious lovers of Hellenism and ancient religions spawned all sorts of strange mutations, superseding their parents' debauchery.

So Paneas became to Pan worship what the Vatican is to Catholicism, or Mecca to Islam.

It was Alexander who named the area Paneas and made it the holy city of the Greek god Pan. It was an easy transition. Previously the goddess Asherah had been worshipped here, and without going into too much detail, the whole religious experience was one of eroticism and unbridled sexuality. Asherah and Pan were fertility gods, responsible for growth, the harvest and new life. Their worshippers aimed to be one with them and please them through, you guessed it, acts of fertility. The earliest references to the religious experience of 'being in the spirit' is the word 'orgy', which describes an ecstatic release, losing yourself and connecting to the god. These large gatherings to worship the fertility gods would make today's hedonistic displays look very tame indeed. The simplest way to understand the central idea of the Pan mythology was that he would go into the underworld, copulate with his mistresses the nymphs and that, quite literally, the sperm of Pan would be the rain. Sorry, I know it's all a bit icky, but this was how it was in the minds of the ancient Greeks.

You only have to do a Google image search for pictures of this little goatee god and you will see the central issue as that of his sexuality. The vast majority of the pictures and statues are simply inappropriate as they tend to show Pan as having a huge erect phallus. Usually in the earliest statues the actual torso of Pan would be rather small, but his penis would be very large, making it the main focus of their worship. They would bow to it, kiss it and gratify themselves and each other with it. Yes, I know this is a Christian book and for many readers this subject matter may make you feel a bit uncomfortable, but I do have a point, so please don't bail on me just yet. This was the darkest, dirtiest, seediest little section of Israel and certainly no place for a good God-fearing Jew. Its name was changed to Caesarea Paneas or Philippi in AD 14 under Philip II, son of Philip the Tetrarch. He named it Caesarea (in honour of the Roman Emperor Caesar Augustus); the Philippi bit was added partly to distinguish it from Caesarea Maritima on the Mediterranean coast, but also to claim it as his own.

At the foot of Mount Hermon in Caesarea Philippi, there is a grotto which has been amazingly preserved to the present day and is still known as Pan's grotto. To Greek and Jew alike this area had an interesting and widely known nickname. It was known as 'the Gates of Hades'.

Hades or the underworld was understood to be a dark and shadowy place, the realm of departed spirits. The Greeks believed that this was geographically beneath the earth. When people of the ancient world saw openings in the earth they presumed these were doorways into that underworld, gates to another realm. More than any other area in Israel during the Second Temple period, Caesarea Philippi was considered the portal to, and Pan's grotto the gates, of Hades.

The worship of Pan was highly erotic and extremely debauched – it would make the Las Vegas strip, home to the most notorious strip clubs, seem tame in comparison. The normal procedure would be for the priests and priestesses of Pan to bring out the sacred goats in heat and to openly have sexual relations with each other and also with the goats in a frenzied belief that this would bring about fertility of the land and the flocks. Caesarea Philippi had a population of approximately 30,000 including the surrounding areas, and the worshippers would gather in their droves to be a part of this ceremony. In this atmosphere of intense, brazen, unbridled sexuality, the worshippers would then respond and begin to do likewise, turning Pan's grotto into a mass orgy site with worshippers having sexual relations with each other and with the goats, women with women, men with men, men and women together, men and goats, women and goats, men and women with goats. Unsurprisingly, this was known as 'pandemonium'.

It is hard for us to get our heads around such a scene and to understand how or why such an understanding and practice of worship could have come about. Psychologist Havelock Ellis notes that in ancient religions 'men may become animals and animals may become men', and so in this vein to the ancient Greeks there was 'no shame or degradation in the notion of sexual relations between man and animals,' because 'animals were not considered inferior beings, separated by a great gulf'. Animals were considered to 'possess power in some instances making them superior to men'. Herodotus, speaking of the worship of Pan said, 'It happened that within this country, to my remembrance, and was indeed universally notorious that the goats had indecent and public communications with the women.' Caesarea Philippi was a very dark place indeed.

This was a place that good Jewish boys and girls from Galilee or the orthodox triangle simply did not visit – they knew that if they were ever to get caught there, they would be in very serious trouble with their parents. It was the ancient equivalent of being caught at a porn convention. However, the scriptures inform us that Jesus begins to walk, together with his disciples towards Caesarea Philippi. The journey would have been approximately eighteen miles and, amazingly, the scriptures don't give us even a hint of a whisper of what was talked about on that journey along the Via Maris towards that notorious place. I like to think that Jesus didn't say anything on purpose.

Type A people get driven crazy when they don't know exactly what is going to happen. 'So where are we going? When are we going to get there? Will I be able to plug in my hair straighteners?' Sometimes we just have to go with the flow. I can imagine those teenage boys walking that dusty high road and chattering amongst themselves under their breath. 'Surely not...' Peter says to James. 'He can't be taking us there. Can he?' whispers Levi. 'He wouldn't, right? I mean, come on now, he's heard the stories?' retorts Nathanael. 'Dude, if your mum finds out you are soooooo dead', chuckles John. All the while Jesus keeps walking and I don't think he had acquired signed permission slips from the disciples' mums and dads beforehand either!

The scriptures say he enters the region of Caesarea Philippi. Now you might be thinking, 'Well, hang on a second then, if he's just in the region, who's to say he goes anywhere near Pan's cesspit?' My question to your question would in turn be, 'If he didn't, then the eighteen-mile hike was a bit of a waste of time, don't you think? Why spend all that time and energy getting there if Jesus isn't going to show them the darkness of that place?'

Amazingly it is in this setting of idolatry that Jesus asks them the question 'Who do people say I am?'

When Jesus came to the region of Caesarea Philippi, he asked his disciples, 'Who do people say the Son of Man is?'

They replied, 'Some say John the Baptist; others say Elijah; and still others, Jeremiah or one of the prophets.'

'But what about you?' he asked. 'Who do you say I am?'

Simon Peter answered, 'You are the Christ, the Son of the living God.'

Matthew 13:16

Peter's statement was a very interesting one when you take it in the Jewish context into which it was spoken. It is just not very Jewish to use the term 'the living God', unless you are specifically trying to differentiate between what is true and what is false, what is living and what is dead. First of all this is radical, because Peter is seeing something in the Spirit that up to this point had not been seen. Nor had the prophets of old comprehended that the Messiah was not simply another deliverer like Moses, or King David, albeit a super-duper deliverer, but that actually he was in a very real sense the son and the likeness of God – what they would come to understand as the fullness of the godhead in bodily form. No one had heard anything like this before. No one had guessed that God himself would put on an earthsuit and the infinite put on finite form. The all-powerful made himself vulnerable. This was earthshattering.

What is more is that, if he is differentiating the real from the false, it stands to reason that the false was right in front of them, which means that Jesus has taken these impressionable guys into the darkest seediest region of the Holy Land and exposed them to a disgusting, degrading display for one who is not 'the living God'. Why would he do that? I believe that Jesus wanted his followers to see the depths of the darkness of sin and just how low human nature could fall. Jesus did not hide his followers away or protect them in ivory towers – they were not to curl up in cloisters or gather in ghettos. No, they were to step out into the world with a fire in their hearts, blazing as cities on a hill for all to see.

Something incredibly profound happens here. With pandemonium going on around them, Peter recognises who Jesus is and in turn Jesus is going to reveal to Peter who Peter really is: 'And I tell you that you are Peter, and on this rock I will build my church, and the gates of Hades will not overcome it.' When we meet face to face with Jesus and a revelation of who he really is explodes within our hearts, we in turn find out who we really are. Jesus changes our name and our identity and we are never the same again.

We find in the book of Genesis Abraham's grandson Jacob, a schemer, a self made man, fighting for everything he gets in life, tricking everyone around him, until the night when he comes face to face with God. The scriptures say that a wrestling match follows and Jacob does a pretty good job. He tells the Lord that he will not let him go. God ends the fight with a gentle jab to the hip that leaves Jacob limping the rest of his life. However, Jacob has been changed, transformed. God changes his name to Israel. He is no longer a schemer, but a prince with God. Whenever we come face to face with God, we are transformed.

The name Peter (*Petros*) means 'stone'. Jesus is using

a concrete, earthy image to convey a profound spiritual point. It is clear that Peter, bless his heart, had a problem with consistency. One moment he is promising Jesus that he will follow him to the death, then he's cutting a guard's ears off, then he's scared of a servant girl. He is anything but firm as a rock and yet God has an uncanny way of seeing us as how we can be, rather than how we currently are. He calls things that are not as though they were, according to Romans 4:19. Yahweh says, 'Childless Abram, I'm going to call you "father of nations", scaredy cat Gideon, I'm going to call you "mighty warrior", weak, inconsistent Peter, I'm going to call you a rock. Not only that, I'm going to use you mightily to build and advance my kingdom, starting with that revelation that my Father in heaven revealed to you.'

Catholic tradition, commenting on this verse, interprets Jesus' words as saying that the rock on which he will 'build [his] church' is Peter himself. From this we see the doctrine of apostolic succession, with Peter being the first Pope. In one sense there is truth here – Peter opened the doors wide for the kingdom when he stood up on the day of Pentecost and revival broke out in a powerful way.

Protestant tradition says, 'No, you've got it wrong. The rock is the revelation that Peter has had.' The church, the Jesus movement, the revolution needed to rock planet earth, will be built on the truth that Jesus is the son of the living God. He is the Messiah, he is the way the truth and life and everything that that entails. Much truth can be found in this interpretation too.

There is an interesting nuance in the Greek in that when Jesus says on this rock, he uses the word *petra,* not *petros.* *Petra* has a very different significance in that, unlike *petros*, meaning rock or stone, *petra* means a huge rock. The rock of Gibraltar, which has an entire city and community built on it, is a *petra*.

However, I think we may have missed something by not understanding the geographical context of what is happening here. Pan's Grotto was a huge *petra*, with a large gaping cavern that looked like a monster's mouth. Is it possible, that just maybe, Jesus was saying in subtext that his church would be built in the darkest places and that it would overcome the worst kinds of confusion and deception? That there was nowhere too lost, and nothing too strong to stand against his movement?

The disciples must have felt they'd had the air knocked out of them as they realised that their calling would not be a calling of comfort, to nice cosy Capernaum or glorious Galilee, but to the very bowels of human existence, to step into the flames and pull the dying out, to venture into the lion's den. Was Jesus suggesting that, just possibly, his church would be a violent rescue mission, rather than all about plush seats, ministry partner's privileges, lights, cameras and action? That it would be life on the edge, breathtaking, awe-inspiring, adrenaline-pumping life, advancing the King and his kingdom, even here – on this rock!

We are not called to hide from the devil. I want my churches and the followers and disciples of Jesus that he has put me in a position of leadership with to see sin in all of its ugliness, to see it up close, where the glimmer and shine is gone, the masks have fallen and the reality screams out, vomits in front of them the truth. The glamour of pornography quickly disappears when someone sees the suicide note of the actress who can no longer go on.

The corporate sin of greed that allows me to buy cheap chocolate or fashionable clothes at the expense of children slaving away in the sun is simply not acceptable. Until we face the realities, it is very easy to, as the Delirious? song says, live in 'a kingdom of comfort, where I am king.' I never thought about the children being sold for the price of my latte until I met some of them. We are called to go out and do something about all of this. Politics will not provide the answer, science has failed miserably, humanism has caused the worst world wars and bloodshed imaginable. The only answer is Jesus.

I was on my way to train to become either a writer or an actor – those were the options that I believed would be the trajectory of my life. I was studying A-level History, English Literature and Theatre Studies and absolutely loving it. God had turned my life around, I was now healthy, and he had put great friends in my life. There was nothing wrong with what I was thinking about doing with my life, and I am sure that whatever path we take when our hearts are in the right place God will use us in it. However it would soon become clear that God had something else in mind.

In May 1998 I was able to accompany my father to Mexico City. I had never seen poverty, not real poverty anyway. Stepping out of the airport into the hot, suffocating city, feeling the pollution fill my lungs and seeing children sleeping rough on the streets assaulted my every emotion. We pulled up at a fried chicken place and while waiting in the queue I felt a gentle tug on the back of my t-shirt. Looking around I saw a little girl, possibly as old as eight, though I remember thinking she was much younger. Her face had been terribly burnt. I was shocked. Our hosts informed us, through their extensive work with people who had made both the streets and sewers of Mexico City their home, that it was very likely that her mother had burnt her face to evoke greater sympathy, causing people to be more willing to part with their loose change. I couldn't believe what my eyes were witnessing or what my ears were hearing and my heart, which had been calloused by years of living in a world of comfort, finally began to break. My world began to spiral and the trajectory of my life would never be the same again.

God has called us to the darkest place to blaze his light and set the world on fire. Light is supposed to shine in darkness. We must face the truth that this rock must be taken and that hell itself can't stop us – the Church. We are the answer, people!

So is there any evidence that could back up that this is indeed what Jesus is saying?

'The gates of Hades will not prevail against it!' the declaration rings out. In Greek mythology Hades was the brother of Zeus and Poseidon and ruled the underworld, something he seemed to be a bit put out by. It didn't have views anywhere near as nice as Olympus, you see! Hades became synonymous with the place he ruled and the Hellenistic Jews began to refer to Sheol as Hades. As we have seen, dark shadowy places, such as caves, caverns or any type of opening in the earth, came to be known as gateways to the underworld, and Pan's Grotto in particular was known as 'the Gates of Hades'. Whether in legend or reality, it was said that smoke gases would rise up from the grotto and it was believed that these were departed spirits escaping the underworld.

In Luke's version of these events, Jesus goes on to turn to the crowd and say 'If anyone would come after me, he must deny himself and take up his cross daily and follow me. For whoever wants to save his life will lose it, but whoever loses his life for me will save it. What good is it for a man to gain the whole world, and yet lose or forfeit his very self?'

Who were the 'crowd'? They weren't the Pharisees! They wouldn't be caught dead in the vicinity of Caesarea Philippi; they weren't the Sadducees, nor the religious Samaritans. They were the Hellenists, the Pan worshippers. The Greek word used for 'said' is actually *lego* which means to cry out, to shout and affirm. Some people don't like to think of Jesus as shouting, but the truth is that meek and mild Jesus was a man of fire and intensity – he was no stoic philosopher. Jesus was passionate and very much at ease with showing his emotions. You do not get mistaken for the wild-eyed fiery prophet Elijah without being a very passionate individual. Jesus cries out to the crowd at the top of his voice because he desperately wants to see them free. He isn't Bible-bashing them, rather he is snatching them from the flames.

Jesus says 'if anyone' – isn't that awesome! There is no one so bad that he cannot love them, no one so dirty that his blood cannot wash them whiter than snow! But we must lose our rights, give up the fight and let him do what only he can do. Once again we must die to ourselves.

He then turns to his disciples, who are probably feeling pretty uncomfortable by now, thinking, 'Jesus, for goodness' sake keep your voice down. We're not in Capernaum any more. I mean it's one thing talking like that around the Pharisees but, come on, you're really embarrassing us! This is Herod's town! Keep your voice down.' Then Jesus says, 'If anyone is ashamed of me and my words, the Son of Man will be ashamed of him when he comes in his glory and in the glory of the Father and of the holy angels.' It's one thing raising our arms in church, singing to Jesus, declaring our faith when we are around others of like mind. It's a different story when we are amongst those who are agnostic, or completely hostile to what we believe. Often we don't do ourselves any favours with the way we present ourselves but still, we are called to be unashamed as we declare the truth in love.

Truth and Love

Not easy, right? But without both we get into a lot of trouble. All truth and no love = legalism. Pains in the blessed *ass*urance! All love and no truth = wishy-washy, anything-goes emptiness.

We have to balance the seesaw if we want to impact people's lives. Jesus never asked for a hand without first touching a heart. He never asked people to change without first showing them the change they could be. He never asked anyone to respect him and his message without first pouring out love and respect to them, and it mattered not whether they were prostitute or politician, priest or pimp. Jesus loved and from that foundation he could speak the truth. And again his voice rings out: 'Be like me!'

Perhaps the young Philip who would become the future evangelist and revivalist was with Jesus in this moment. He started off as an administrator working behind the scenes within the early church (Acts 6:5). It wasn't a particularly glamorous profession. But he went on to do some extraordinary things, proclaiming Christ in Samaria and performing miracles there, and even initiating the advancement of Christianity on the continent of Africa in his encounter with the Ethiopian eunuch (Acts 8:26–40). Even so, following these astonishing beginnings to Philip's ministry, we don't really hear any more about this remarkable New Testament figure. However, according to tradition, he continued to shake the world around him with the power of the gospel. Years later history tells us that Philip moved to Hierapolis.

The ancient city of Hierapolis made Caesarea Philippi look like a theme park by comparison. This was the Las Vegas of the Roman world! It was a gambling centre and was well known for being a place of extreme vice. It was about six miles from Laodicea, one of the seven churches we read about in the book of Revelation. Hierapolis was the site of the temple to the god Apollo, and it was here that the Greek god of music, prophecy, and light was worshipped.

The temple was impressive, with beautiful architecture and a grand fountain called Nymphia, which was a constant reminder to the people that Apollo was their source of life. The whole area between Hierapolis in the valley, up to Colossae in the mountains was known for its springs. In Hierapolis, right next to the temple, was a mysterious opening in the ground, a small cave large enough for a person to enter, known as the Plutonium. Pluto was the Roman version of Hades, so this was also considered a Gate of Hades. Poisonous gases emanated from the hole and instantly killed any animals that wandered in. An enclosed area of 2,000 square metres was cordoned off around the entrance, which historians say was covered by a thick layer of suffocating gas so powerful that it would almost instantly kill everyone who dared to set foot within this area.

The priests made huge amounts of money by selling various birds and other kinds of animals for worshippers to release into the poisonous gas so that they could see for themselves how deadly this cordoned off area really was. They also made money by charging fees to allow the worshippers to ask questions of the oracle of Pluto. The priests of Apollo would then astonish the crowds by entering the cave and then emerging shortly after unharmed. They seem to have had either a remarkable ability to hold their breath or they had some other means of breathing fresh air. As far as the worshippers were concerned they seemed to have power over death!

Hierapolis, like most beachheads of Hellenism, had an impressive theatre, which communicated through its architecture as well as its activities the people's devotion to their gods and goddesses. One can still see the images of gods and goddesses depicted in the ornately carved stones. But Hierapolis' greatest architects were not people, nor were its most impressive or lasting buildings made from rocks. Its greatest tourist attraction was its hot springs. The baths complex of the Hierapolis was one of the largest in all of Asia Minor; it allowed hundreds of people to bathe at the same time. People from distant regions came to soak in warm baths and seek healing for arthritis, skin diseases, and even abdominal problems.

It is believed that the city didn't have walls surrounding it and what is left of the entrance to the city, is simply a gate complex of two gigantic towers and three arches that opened onto a paved street about a mile and a half long.

These stand as a testimony to the city's former majesty. What is most important is not the gate's size or architecture, however, but what it represented. Like most city gates of the ancient world, the gates of the Hierapolis expressed the people's devotion to their gods. For Hierapolis, that god was the Roman emperor Domitian, one of the first emperors to declare himself to be divine. Thus anyone who entered the Domitian Gate was, in a sense, acknowledging that Domitian was god, their provider and protector whom they would honour and obey above all others.

Philip, living in Hierapolis, would have had to choose whether to serve and worship Caesar (in this case, Domitian) or to serve and worship the God of Israel. He refused to recognise the authority of Domitian. Philip's stance was 'I only know one God and Lord of all the earth and he is not Domitian, not Vespasian, not Augustus Caesar, his name is Jesus and only he is worthy of our praise.' Philip and his children stood fast in their declaration that Jesus alone is Lord of Lords and King of Kings, and they paid the ultimate price.

For more than six years it is believed that Philip and his family came and went into the city, doing great works, signs and wonders and seeing many lives transformed by the power of the gospel, until one day someone turned him in. The authorities presented Philip with a choice: 'Either recognise Domitian as Lord and bow your knee to him or we will crucify you. Your fate is in your hands – chose carefully.' He replied that he could never turn his back on his Lord and Saviour, and his wife and children did the same.

Tradition says that Philip was forced to watch his wife and seven daughters crucified in front of him before finally being hung on a cross to die that slow and painful death himself. High on a hill overlooking Hierapolis are the remains of a small building known as the Martyrium of Philip.

Now you tell me – was that *talmid* just like his Rabbi? Did he follow in his footsteps? Was he covered in his dust?

The very same challenge goes out to us today, more than 2000 years since Jesus of Nazareth made that statement on the rocky dry and dusty roads surrounding the gates of Hades. His voice, rings through the ages and echoes through the centuries. Will you follow me? Will you take up your cross? Will you go into all the world, with my power, my authority, my spirit lifting you, carry you onward? Will you dare to believe that you can be like me?

Will we believe that we can be like our Rabbi? Will we go with his *shmicha*, his authority from heaven, from almighty God, not just parroting what we have heard, but binding and loosing, bringing revelation knowledge straight from the heart of Abba father? Will we go and turn the world upside down like those twelve went and turned the world upside down?

If Jesus could take twelve, in many ways failed individuals, very likely young, inexperienced, untrained, unequipped and do what he did, can you even begin to imagine or fathom, what he could do with each of us if we would just get out of the boat and believe that we can walk with him on the water?

If we would step out, and step up to the plate, If we would be people passionately, desperately chasing after our Rabbi and desiring to be like him, can you imagine the possibilities? Let's not be Essenes, hiding out in religious communes of comfort, or Sadducees, compromising with the world, or Pharisees constantly arguing and hairsplitting over what may be truth, but missing the heartbeat of love. And let's not be Zealots, maybe not murdering with the sword but with our words, so zealous to protect the truth that like Peter we cut off the ears of our listeners and stop people from coming close.

No, it is time for the saints to rise, covered in the Rabbi's dust. For those who know their failings, who know their weaknesses, who have stood in the cold of the night and denied their Rabbi and yet have looked him again square in the eyes and heard him say with love in his voice, 'Feed my lambs, Follow me, be like me, believe in me. I believe in you!'